DYING TO LIVE

Tolly Burkan

with

Mark Bruce Rosin

REUNION PRESS
TWAIN HARTE, CALIFORNIA

ISBN 0-935616-03-9
LIBRARY of CONGRESS CATALOG CARD NUMBER 84-62759

Front cover photo by Richard Drake
Back cover photo by Lynne Jerome

Copies of this book can be purchased at your favorite bookstore or ordered by mail
from the publisher. Mail orders must also include $1.50 for postage and handling.
California residents please add 54¢ sales tax.

Manufactured in the United States of America

REUNION PRESS, INC.
BOX 1738
TWAIN HARTE, CA 95383

Dedicated with love

to

MY MOTHER AND FATHER

who have struggled and grown along with me, and who, in being able to accept me unconditionally, have given me a precious gift.

— **TOLLY BURKAN**

ACKNOWLEDGMENTS

The authors wish to acknowledge everyone mentioned in the book and also Jon Bernoff who brought them together for this collaboration. Thanks also to Peggy Dylan and Cynthia Hoppenfeld for their invaluable support and Elizabeth Crow for her incisive comments.

TOLLY BURKAN WALKING ON GLOWING COALS 1200° F.

INTRODUCTION

Five months ago I walked on fire. Red hot coals to be more exact. A chemical engineer who brought a special thermometer to measure their temperature reported that the instrument began to melt when the heat reached 850 degrees. My feet, however, didn't even blister.

The man who lit the fire for this experience, both literally and metaphorically, was Tolly Burkan. At thirty-six years old, Tolly has been a teacher in the human potential movement for twelve years, in America and also in Europe. The seminar during which I walked on fire was about overcoming fear.

You may well wonder what firewalking could possibly have to do with you. This book, *Dying To Live*, will tell you.

The firewalk that I attended included thirty-nine participants in all, and though few voiced an intention to walk on fire at the beginning of the evening (most said they came to watch others do it), by the evening's end thirty-seven had walked over the eight-foot burning path. (One participant couldn't do it — he had a wooden leg and no amount of courage, he explained, would make it immune from burning; another, a young woman who had come to transcend some private fears, told us she had reached a new level of inner confidence even though she had chosen not to walk across the coals.)

Minutes after I walked across the burning coals, I realized that the experience — amazing though it was — was not important in itself but rather as a concrete example of the ability we all have to do things we may not feel we can do. The knowledge that I was able to do something *that* remarkable made me feel that I was rather remarkable myself. With a new sense of power, I had the confidence to challenge and overcome other more mundane limitations I had been placing on myself for years. Suddenly I was making phone calls I had been afraid to make, tackling projects I had been afraid to tackle, beginning changes in lifestyle that I had postponed because I feared the very process of change.

The success of the firewalk in catalyzing these changes was that much more impressive given my original attitude toward it. Initially I told myself, I was attending the seminar only because I was collaborating on this book with Tolly, and I wanted to be familiar with his work on a first-hand — but not first-foot — basis. In an effort to make certain that I didn't have to endanger my feet, legs, or life just to prove to Tolly — or myself — that I was brave and that I got something out of his work, I told him I was definitely *not* going to walk on fire.

As is his nature, Tolly accepted my stance with good humor and graciousness, and welcomed me to participate on whatever terms made me comfortable.

As the seminar date approached, however, I became increasingly aware of how fundamental the whole subject of fear was to my personality. I had spent the majority of my thirty-six years afraid of one thing or another on almost an hourly basis. If it wasn't fear of disease or accident, it was fear of financial ruin, of making a fool of myself in my eyes or somebody else's, of confrontation or lack of confrontation, of not being happy or of being too happy. As I went over these fears, I began to realize that if I were to be honest with myself, I should not go to Tolly's seminar merely as a writer involved in a project; I should go as a full participant who could derive a great deal of benefit from learning about overcoming fear.

With this in mind, I realized that my fear of walking on fire was no greater or less great than a hundred other fears I'd had in my life. My basic assumption had always been, *"Well, maybe he (or she) can do it, but I know I can't."* I could see the absurdity of clinging to this view even when I knew I had no real reason to be afraid. In this instance, I knew that even if I couldn't understand *how* I could walk on fire, it would be no more difficult for me than it had been for the thousands Tolly had already led across the hot coals.

Still, I was not at all sure that I could — or would — walk on fire.

But I did. And the reason I did has a lot to do with Tolly Burkan. Tolly didn't give me courage to do it; he put me in touch with my own courage. Part of what gave me and the other members of the seminar the ability to use our hidden resources was the information he related to us about the nature of our fears and the methods we could adopt to conquer them. The rest had to do with Tolly himself. His humor, his vitality, his energy — his vibrations — are uplifting. His smile radiates a contagious happiness and an acceptance of life. Knowing him today, it's almost impossible to believe that in his first twenty-four years, his self-esteem was so low, his relationships with people — parents, friends, lovers — so traumatic, that twice he tried to kill himself. It was only with intense difficulty that he was finally able to forge loving and respectful relationships, and to emerge as he is now.

Dying To Live is Tolly's autobiography, the story of the incidents and people in his life, and of the discoveries that helped him to survive and to evolve into the joyful person he is today. Although he has experienced enough personal drama for several dramatic lives, what most attracted me to work on his autobiography with him was not the drama in itself, but the fact that as extreme as his life has been, I find in it an oversized blueprint of my own life. Mercifully, my life has not actually been on the brink as his has been, and my negative emotions and conflicts have not been so great that they threatened to consume me. But like most people, I've certainly had, and still have, my own struggles in the process of working toward becoming a balanced adult.

Tracing the steps of Tolly's difficult evolution has given me a new and enormous appreciation of the many blessings in my own life. It has also helped me to realize that I, too, have been taking steps along a very definite path, even if sometimes I felt I was standing still. Learning from him the techniques he learned to cope with crises and to overcome obstacles has given me insights into ways I can cope better and use my energy more productively. This is particularly helpful since I've discovered that the process of growing up doesn't end at twenty-one, as I once had thought, or even at thirty-six, but instead will continue, apparently, for as long as I live.

Many of us experience depression and fear more often than we would like to, many of us feel dissatisfaction with the unhappiness or anxiety in which we habitually find ourselves, but we don't know what to do about changing our mental condition and conditioning. *Dying To Live* isn't just a blueprint of a struggle toward maturity, it is a blueprint for the integration of body, mind and spirit. It is the story of how weakness can become strength, how our limitations can be transcended as we learn to love and to trust ourselves and the other people in our lives.

Tolly doesn't give us answers in *Dying To Live;* he tells us about the answers he has found for himself. I believe these can help and inspire others to find their own answers. I know they have already helped me.

—MARK BRUCE ROSIN

In the context of my life, the story contained in this book represents a bizarre wildcard to have been dealt. Only now do I feel emotionally mature enough and spiritually aware enough to share the personal details of it. The title *Dying To Live* is more than just a spiritual metaphor; I actually had a life after death experience. The *Daily News* headline on the back cover is linked to a drama that took me seventeen years to put into words. I always knew the story had to be shared, and this is the time.

— TOLLY BURKAN

1

In 1973, by the time I was twenty-four, I had lived the better part of five years sailing from ocean to ocean on the world's largest luxury liners — the S. S. Michelangelo, the S. S. Rafaello, the S. S. Leonardo Da Vinci, the S. S. Rotterdam — as a social director and professional magician. With less than two hours of work required of me most days and some days going by work-free, my job was very much like a long and expensive vacation.

One night I was aboard the S. S. Rotterdam at a party thrown by Taylor Caldwell to celebrate the publication of her novel, *The Captains and the Kings*. Diamonds glittered on many throats and wrists as guests consumed an endless banquet of shrimp, lobster and caviar. The ballroom was an appropriate setting for such opulence, with its etched copper dance floor, thirty-foot high sculpted ceiling, panoramic picture windows and a carpeted staircase that wound its way down from the muraled mezzanine to the main floor where a tuxedoed orchestra played fox-trots and waltzes. All around were garlands of tropical flowers and six-foot ice statues of swans and dolphins. In the center

1

of the buffet, a four-foot ice replica of *The Captains and the Kings* reflected the setting sun.

What I remember most is how little I was able to enjoy myself. I stood near the dance floor in my velvet tuxedo watching the other guests, feeling that despite their laughter and smiling faces, they were just as unhappy as I was, partying on the dead-end street of success because they didn't know where else to go.

Although it was easy for me to see everyone else's apparent folly in life, it was not because I felt I was so much better than anyone else. Quite the contrary. It was because I hated myself, and everywhere I looked I felt people were reflecting back to me the very wretchedness I felt within. I saw myself as a failure, a liar, a fraud. I earned my living as a clown magician, dancing about with a shit-eating grin on my face, pretending to be light-hearted and blithe. Inside, behind the mask I had painted for myself, a mask I had finally come to despise, lurked a depressed, suicidal young man who found life a relentless trap, never producing joy but only confinement and torture — first offering promises and hopes, then dashing them to the ground.

I had often tried to determine how or why I had deteriorated from a bright, ebullient child into a self-loathing creature, and my failure to arrive at any understanding or conclusion only compounded my depression and brought me closer to suicide. In fact, I had become so disenchanted that the only solution to life, I thought, was death.

Only a few weeks before, I had traveled to India in an effort to find "enlightenment," the mysterious spiritual commodity about which I had read and heard so much in metaphysical teachings. Once I found it, I was certain "enlightenment" would give me all the wonderful inner experiences I was seeking. But all I brought back from India were memories of children starving in the streets, poverty so shocking it was hard to believe, and the impression that most Indians dreamed of America, believing that if they could have even a fraction of our wealth they would surely be happy. Indeed, many Indians seemed to think that *every* American lived each day in bliss.

If that were true, the guests at *The Captains and the Kings* party should have been among the most blissful people on earth. But as far as I could see, they weren't any happier than I was. What upset me most was that I had even begun to doubt that enlightenment was possible. And that thought had a devastating effect on me. It meant that all I could hope for now was to continue acquiring money, possessions, achievements and people, and to continue wondering, as I had been — "Isn't there anything *more* than this?"

Several days after the ball I decided to return to that painless place from which we all come. I had tried to kill myself once before, but then it was because I was so overcome by sadness that I had impulsively seized suicide as a way to escape; this time, two years later, I arrived at the decision "rationally." In my 24 years, I had, I reasoned, already finished exploring life's possibilities. I had experienced the best of what life could offer materially and some of the worst it could offer emotionally — divorce, confinement in a mental institution, and the death of two people I dearly loved. Having seen what I considered to be life's boundaries in both directions, life didn't seem worth continuing.

While still aboard ship, in the middle of the Pacific, I calmly dissolved a supply of sleeping pills in half a quart of vodka. The last time, with the help of medical technology, the doctors had brought me back even after my heart had ceased to beat. The memory of the coma and the months I had spent in the hospital made me shudder, but only briefly, before I resolved that this time I would make certain there would be no return to life. I added an assortment of everything in the medicine cabinet — aspirin, three kinds of tranquilizers, sea-sickness medication — to the vodka and sleeping pills and lay down for my final sleep. Three days passed. The crew assumed I was drunk and covered for me as they let me "sleep it off." Soon my heart beat so slowly that blood could not circulate properly in my legs. When my friend, Jim Mapes, finally managed to open the door I had locked from the inside, the tissue in my legs had already begun to decompose. It was the smell that had made him break into the room.

Again doctors set to work on me. Needles and tubes, wires and machines, all sought to stop my final retreat. I remember none of it; I slept the sleep of the comatose, teetering on the brink of no return.

2

Three weeks later, as I lay on the sofa-bed in the living room of my parents' house in Parsippany, New Jersey, following my second attempt at suicide, I found myself disoriented by the tasks in front of me: having to adjust to the fact that I was, indeed, still alive, and the renewed compulsion I felt to make sense of my first 24 years of life. Crushed and flattened, I wondered what had brought me to this absurd point — I didn't know how to live but obviously I didn't know how to die, either — and I wondered if any good could come from the suffering I had brought upon myself and those around me. The task of going on seemed monumental, especially in my state of self-pity and confusion.

I had been taken off the ship in Panama. My parents had flown down from New Jersey and had made arrangements for me to be transported by ambulance to the intensive care unit of an American hospital in the Canal Zone. When I finally opened my eyes, I thought my legs had been amputated. They weren't; only paralyzed and numb. I found no joy in the discovery that

I was not dead. The word that burned in my mind was, Why?

Now that I was in my parents' house, my nineteen-year-old brother, Barry, my closest friend, gave me the clue with a quiet comment he made. "Obviously, you're supposed to be here," he told me. "If it was your time to die surely by now you would've been dead." Clearly I *was* meant to be here; I had been thinking the same thing since I first woke up in the hospital in Panama. But the question still remained, Why? And why was I so addicted to pain and to hurting my family as well?

3

My parents divorced right before my second birthday, and I have no early memory of my father. My mother, Eileen, an intelligent, attractive woman — tall, blonde and slim, with bright blue eyes and a vivacious personality — was a model before becoming pregnant with me. She remarried when I was three, and Ted, her second husband, the only father I've ever known, adopted me and gave me his name even before I entered nursery school. Smart, handsome, trim, with thick black hair and soulful brown eyes, he has always had the slightly removed air of a professor.

My father was devoted to our family and had a generally quiet disposition, but he also had a quick temper and frequently solved child-rearing problems with a raised voice and a strap. He established early on that where matters of my conduct were concerned, he was to be taken seriously the first time around. The message I received from him was, "Consider my needs before your own." Approval seemed to be forthcoming only if I could guess and do what he expected of me. There was an invisible line over which I could not go without making him furious. And since, especially as a young child, I was extremely hungry for attention, I crossed this line many times — with disastrous results. Even though I knew the consequences, sometimes I would resort to anything, good or bad, to get my parents to focus on me.

When my father dragged me into my bedroom to hit me, I remember hoping that my screams would bring my mother. But they didn't. By not objecting to my father's use of corporal punishment, by always demanding that I act in a way that would make both her and my father proud — and crying if I didn't — my mother also gave me no margin for what she considered misbehaving. Although they certainly didn't intend this, my parents' extreme treatment communicated to me that I had very little worth and no right to have needs and demands at all. I had no idea then how much they loved me.

The sanctuary of my childhood was Grandma's house. Fortunately it was only a few blocks away. My grandmother had taken care of me when my mother's first marriage was falling apart, and we formed a bond that lasted until her death. Whenever the stress of my own home became unbearable, I would seek refuge at Grandma's, eating her special lentil-barley soup and playing Canasta, which she taught me when I was three. "Your brothers are my grandsons," she told me as I grew older, "but you are my son."

When I was five years old something happened that I thought would solve all my problems: I was given a magic set by Uncle Harold, my father's younger brother. Harold, who was both a doctor and a magician — the magic had provided the money for his medical education — had dazzled me with magic tricks for as long as I could remember. I was thrilled to have him teaching me how to perform tricks myself. I soon learned that magic isn't only accomplished through sleight of hand and special props: the magician's primary means of deception is his ability to lie impeccably and to misdirect his audience's attention. Magi-

AGE ELEVEN

AGE TWELVE

Parsippany's Bruce Burkan, a witty magician.

AGE THIRTEEN

cians have to be expert psychologists, I discovered, watching people closely at all times; their job is to manipulate minds as well as objects.

Performing magic was even more enthralling to me than watching magic tricks had been, and by the time I was nine, I was amazing adults with my adept prestidigitation. To my delight, I had found a perfectly acceptable way of being in the spotlight as much as I wanted. Gratified by the attention I was receiving and, on a deeper level, sensing, even then, the in-

AGE FOURTEEN

AGE FIFTEEN

credible power that performing magic was giving to me and would continue to give to me throughout my life, I pursued my new craft with diligence. By age fourteen, I started to earn money as a magician by performing for local parties and organizations. By age sixteen I decided it was going to be my career, and I changed from being Bruce Burkan, the magician, to Tolly the Clown Magician.

AGE SIXTEEN

Magic and clowning seemed like the ideal combination to me: of all my accomplishments, the one I valued most was my ability to make people laugh. I felt best about myself when I created laughter, and I felt that by being a clown I was actually expressing my true identity — the playful child part of myself. Instinctively I knew that next to love, laughter was the most healthy state in which a person could live, and hearing other people laugh always soothed me. But even with the many rewards generated by my career, by the time I was eighteen I had already begun to think about killing myself.

I had finished high school with honors and, yielding to advice from all sides that I could not be a magic clown for the rest of my life, I reluctantly enrolled at Rutgers University to study a more "realistic" profession: dentistry. Academic and social success came as easily to me in college as it had in high school. But in spite of my intellectual ability, my popularity with young women and my financial independence (by my first year of college, I was turning down at least twice as many bookings as I was able to accept), I was not at all comfortable with the prospect of being an adult, or, at least, an adult as I perceived adults to be. Every day seemed to bring greater and greater anxiety. At first I thought this anxiety was caused by my fear of growing up. Soon, however, I began to suspect that something was radically wrong with me.

One day, during my first year of college, I was sitting in my room doing homework when I noticed my mind constantly wandering. No matter how hard I tried to concentrate on the book in my hands, my mind refused to cooperate. Suddenly my hands began to tremble. Somewhere from within myself I was watching all this happen and feeling absolutely horrified. Within moments I was sobbing beyond control. As perspiration began drenching my clothes, I suddenly released a scream, picked up a ceramic teapot and hurled it at the wall. It exploded in a barrage of tinkling slivers. Appalled by what I was seeing myself do and fearing someone in my family would come to find out what was going on, I proceeded to pile all the furniture in the room against the door in an attempt to barricade myself in. No one was at home, though, and so I sat there alone for hours, struggling to regain my composure. When I finally did begin to feel better, I tidied the room and never mentioned the incident to anyone. From that moment, however, I *knew* something was drastically wrong with me, and I spent fruitless months trying to figure out what it was. My first serious thoughts of suicide were born in those months.

In an effort to vanquish these thoughts, I became engaged to my girl friend, Valerie. I was hoping that marriage was the ingredient that, once provided, would somehow make my life acceptable to me. At nineteen, Valerie was extraordinarily beautiful. She was also intelligent, warm, and very practical. Her stability held the promise of being an anchor for me, too. We met when we were sixteen at the public library where we worked as volunteers. While repairing books and shelving the circulation, we fell in love. We were intense talkers and we talked about everything, excited to find in each other intellectual playmates who could bring the conversation above what we considered the usual teenage drivel.

I also loved Valerie's family, and this added to the attraction I saw in our marriage. Valerie's brother, Teddy, was then my best friend. A year younger than Valerie and myself, he was tall, slender and fair like his sister, but where she was conservative and cautious, he had an irrepressible sense of adventure. Their father, Paul, an extremely affectionate and joyful man, took an immediate liking to me and I soon felt he loved me as much as he did his own children. His wife, Dolores, was a keen observer of life and I delighted in her witty and sharply intelligent conversation. I cared for and respected them all — and admired their happiness and closeness so much that I hoped my marriage to Valerie, in making me part of their family, would also miraculously transform me into a happier person.

But I knew on some unadmitted level that my hope was futile.

Although I enjoyed myself many times during the first two years Valerie and I dated each other, by the time we were engaged, my intermittent anxiety and depression had given way to terror. Of the many things I talked about to Valerie, Teddy and Dolores, the one thing I never mentioned to any of them was how deeply frightened and disturbed I was. They knew me only as the facade I presented to the outside world — that of a happy and outgoing young man — which meant that they did not know me at all. And this added to my isolation and growing discomfort.

About this time I also began re-examining an event that had taken place when I was eleven and both of my parents had been hospitalized with hepatitis. While in the hospital, they retained a housekeeper to look after me and my three brothers, Wayne, Barry and Lee, who were, respectively, ages seven, six and one. The housekeeper's complaints about my frenzied activity, demanding personality and go-for-the-throat temper tantrums resulted in my parents taking me to a psychiatrist as soon as they got back from the hospital. They were so physically weak, and so desperate to keep the woman, they felt it would be best to have a doctor work things out with me.

I was so upset at the prospect of being taken to a psychiatrist that when my parents led me into his office, I tore pictures from his walls, kicked him in his shins and attacked him like a mad dog, ripping his sports jacket and leaving him disheveled in my wake. I told my parents I would never go back. When I changed my mind two weeks later, I was shocked that the doctor agreed to see me. I went for six months. I brought him pictures and told him stories and he listened. Since he never really spoke, I eventually got bored and wanted to discontinue, but my parents pressured me to stay. Finally they gave in to my complaints, and the sessions ended.

At the time, I never really made much of this episode, but seven years later, when I was eighteen, the idea of having been taken to a psychiatrist began to prey on my mind. I was also increasingly disturbed by the fact that physically I was a slow maturer, with a high voice and no body hair. Taunts of "faggot" by my peers in gym class seered to the core of my being. I became haunted by thoughts that I was not masculine enough and fears that I never would be. I thought of going back to a psychiatrist, but I didn't need a psychiatrist to tell me what I was already certain of myself: I was mentally ill.

During my engagement to Valerie, I began to feel that I was accumulating symbols of success, but that nothing I acquired or accomplished had any real substance. Despite the optimistic way I acted, I did not feel optimistic. I was dominated by and eventually obsessed with the thought that there was something terribly wrong with me. I even lost my delight in performing magic. No matter how much energy I put into mystifying and engaging people, I still felt frightened and uncomfortable. While I was acting bright about the future, even while trying to brighten the lives of hospital patients with my magic clowning, inside I felt something very dark was lurking around a bend in the road of my life.

Sleepless nights soon turned into unending nightmares as I looked around and saw the many things I had, but knew they weren't enough. Not knowing what was missing was driving me slowly mad; not knowing why I wasn't happy made me increasingly depressed. I had always had an abundance of energy and a compassionate nature, and wherever I saw an opportunity to use my energy constructively — and get some approval — I did so. I was an Eagle Scout, an honor student, and, as a result of my extensive volunteer work in the library, in hospitals, and for local organizations, a prominent young citizen. The newspapers constantly carried my picture and wrote about my good deeds and my success as a performer. My mother, as attractive as ever, was selected as Mrs. New Jersey, "Mother of the Year," and a finalist in the 1967 Mrs. America Pageant. Living in the spotlight of this contest for over a year intimidated me into never "misbehaving," and this further discouraged me from showing the volatile and depressed side of my personality to anyone. Since I had practiced deception constantly as a magician, I was a master of it: everyone was convinced that I was happy, especially now that I was engaged.

But I had already begun to look at my engagement as just one more empty symbol of success. The more of these symbols I accumulated, the more I felt I knew what adulthood had in store for me, and the less I wanted to continue the hoax that I was living. As I looked at my parents and their friends, I saw nothing in their lives that I didn't already have or couldn't get if I worked for it. All around me I saw stress, competitiveness, insecurity, and insensitivity. Many of the adults I knew seemed

Newark News Photo

AGE EIGHTEEN

to spend the majority of their time searching, struggling, lamenting, pretending and blaming. Even those adults I most admired seemed bridled by the trappings of success and the necessities of the work world. Nowhere did I find someone I would have liked to be like, someone whose condition I envied, whose career I felt I could enter.

My own parents, who ran a real estate office from our home on Littleton Road, seemed to be on an endless treadmill, working day and night to support our family. Unbeknownst to Mrs. New Jersey's admiring public, neither she nor my father were, in my opinion, very happy. Working seven days a week, there never seemed to be enough time or money to bring them all the things they desired in life. What made matters worse was that whenever my parents and I tried to communicate, we wound up fighting, so ultimately I gave up the idea of even trying to communicate with them.

My aversion to fighting with my parents was strengthened by my mother's reference, whenever I would disagree with her and become angry, to me being "just like my father" — meaning my birth father, the man she had divorced. She always spoke of him as being unbalanced, and I took her at her word. I assumed that any man who had been so unfortunate as to ruin his marriage to a wonderful woman like her must have been crazy. So every angry feeling I had, whether expressed or suppressed, was further confirmation to me that I was just as unbalanced as he was, probably more so.

It wasn't only shame that kept me from telling Valerie and her family about my secret problems, although that was a large part of it. As the Magic Clown I was a local folk hero and felt obliged to live up to my public image, which certainly meant hiding any signs of mental unbalance. But I also felt that the torment I carried inside me was so great and so urgent it created a huge black abyss that would threaten the well-being of anybody brought too close. I was already distanced from Valerie's family by another secret — the sexual relationship Valerie and I went to great lengths to hide. This in itself created a great pressure on me and, I think, on Valerie as well. Its very secrecy kept it from being fulfilling: Valerie constantly ruminating on the fact that the good sisters at her alma mater, Morris Catholic High School, would never approve (it was shocking enough that she was engaged to a Jewish boy), and me feeling burdened by the weight of yet another guilty secret.

My inner turmoil grew until finally, out of sheer frustration over my inability to fend off feelings of hopelessness, I began to think seriously about killing myself. Not knowing where to turn, I reluctantly sought a psychiatrist. Unfortunately, I found in him a prime example of everything that disgusted me about the human condition: he chain-smoked cigarettes, had a nervous twitch, and rarely took his eyes off his wrist watch. Judging that he suffered from his own problems, I tried another psychiatrist, who also did not impress me; the fan in his office made such a racket that I felt he heard very little of what I was saying because I was almost whispering and he never asked me to speak louder.

Although suicide seemed more and more a real possibility to me, a fear of the unknown kept me bound to the life I now so despised. Shortly after my nineteenth birthday, I conceived an alternative plan. My sick mind decided to run away, change my name and attempt to start over.

4

It was a disastrous plan from the start, since the cause of my problems was the very "me" I was taking with me, but in my deluded desperation, I concocted a scheme that would enable me to escape from New Jersey to California and to change my identity with forged papers. It seemed like the only possible choice if I didn't want to kill myself. I felt that I simply couldn't continue to live the life of Bruce Tolly Burkan; in order to continue living, maybe to find some happiness, I would have to be a completely new person in a completely new environment, where nobody had any expectations of me and where I couldn't disappoint anybody no matter what I did. I didn't know what I wanted to do that I needed this freedom for, because I felt so restrained by the role I had created for myself that I didn't even know what my true feelings and desires were anymore. All I knew was that I had finally become more negative than positive, and the only solution seemed to be to leave my life behind.

I couldn't simply run away, however, because it would have

been very embarrassing to Mrs. New Jersey and, furthermore, it might be assumed that I had been kidnapped. In any event, I didn't want people looking for me. So I decided to make it look as if I had drowned. As the plan took shape, I settled on the ocean beach at Asbury Park for the setting of my disappearance. In working out the details, I used every skill of deception I had learned as a magician. If I could pull this off successfully, my disappearance would be my ultimate magic trick.

I decided to execute my scheme in August. Before this, however, I planned to undergo some minor surgery for a bladder infection so it would be covered by my family's medical insurance. My recovery was slower than I expected and as the date approached for my disappearance, I felt apprehensive about my weakened condition. Nevertheless, I moved forward with my plan.

On the morning of August 22, 1967, I packed a picnic lunch and loaded the car for a day's outing. In the trunk I carefully concealed the suitcase I had prepared with new clothes and forged identification papers. My parents were not yet awake as I silently walked through the house, sentimentally looking at all the familiar objects I would never see again.

I was in the living room staring at pictures of my family when my mother's voice startled me.

"Where are you going, Bruce?"

"Valerie and I are going to spend the day at Asbury Park," I said casually, hiding my tears by not turning to face her.

"Don't go in the water," my mother instructed with concern "I know you're a good swimmer, but your body hasn't recovered from the surgery yet."

"Of course I won't," I assured her. "We're just going to lie on the beach, maybe stroll the boardwalk."

I turned to kiss her goodbye. Until that moment, I had always seen her as a steel beam; now she seemed so sweet and fragile. I felt wretched knowing the terrible thing I was about to do, knowing the pain I was about to cause her and everyone she loved. I briefly thought that I might wind up rotting eternally as a result of this, but I said goodbye and left to pick up Valerie.

When I arrived at her house, Valerie was excited about the glorious day we were to spend at the beach. I felt sinister, like an evil creature who had come to stalk Tinker Bell. I feigned lightheartedness, forced myself to be downright jovial, and played the act as if I were performing a magic show.

Towels and suntan lotion were bundled together and soon we were on our way. The weather was ideal and the car radio provided a rock and roll soundtrack for our drive south. For me, it was a horror movie. I suffered alone as we joked and discussed plans for our upcoming marriage. Already the morning seemed endless.

When we neared the beach, I parked the car and we walked the remaining few blocks. Soon we were sprawled on a fuzzy blanket on the sand. The sound of the surf, which had always soothed me, seemed to whisper a cautious warning, trying to dissuade me from playing out the final scene of the script I had written.

Ignoring it completely, I said at the appropriate moment, "Sweetheart, I'll be right back. I have to put money in the parking meter. Then we'll swim a little — "

Valerie was alarmed. "You can't go in the water yet. You're still weak."

"I won't strain myself," I assured her. "We'll just wade, or you can splash me. I'll meet you by the water in a few minutes."

I jumped up, but a wave of dizziness brought me to my knees.

"Are you all right?" Valerie asked.

"Yes, I just got up too fast," I said unconvincingly.

Leaving my clothes, wallet, keys and watch on the blanket, wearing only a bathing suit, I staggered toward the men's room beneath the boardwalk. I felt awful. My head was throbbing and nausea had my stomach in a frenzy. As I entered the men's room, I had to squint to refocus my eyes in the darkness of the cavern that housed lockers, toilets and sinks. A compelling urge to empty my bladder brought me before a grimy urinal reeking of human odors and disinfectant. Relieving myself, I looked down and saw a crimson stream of blood pouring from my trembling body. I was hemorrhaging.

"This is insanity," I thought. "I must stop this plan. I'm ill. I need a doctor."

But although the course upon which I was set was draining the very blood from my being, I would not relent. I was willing to risk Hell rather than return to the life that I thought had brought me so much pain. Feeling like the ultimate victim, I stumbled to my car and unlocked the trunk with a duplicate key I'd hidden under the bumper. Every ounce of my strength was required to lift the suitcase from its hiding place. I dragged it to another locker room where I changed into my new clothes, carefully donning dark glasses and a hat to hide my conspicuous red hair. I folded several thousand dollars I had secretly saved into my pocket.

As I arrived at the bus depot, I knew Valerie would be beginning to wonder where I was. And though I knew she would be concerned and upset, at this point the only person I was really thinking about was myself. A glance at the schedule and then at the clock told me I had an hour to wait. "An hour?" my mind screamed, I was sure I had calculated a mere fifteen minute wait. I then realized I had confused the weekend schedule with the one for mid-week when I had been premeditating today's events. I prayed that this delay would not cause me to miss the California flight I had booked under my assumed name.

My heart was already racing and my head reeling when I suddenly noticed Valerie's beach robe walking toward the depot with determination. "Oh, God," I thought frantically. Trying not to panic, I dragged my suitcase into the men's room and locked myself in a vacant stall. There I waited. Again I had to urinate, and again blood poured from me, turning the water in the toilet red. I was shaking, feverish, and my nerves combined with the

afternoon heat drenched me in perspiration. This was demanding more commitment than anything I had ever done.

After about ten minutes, I left the stall and opened the men's
room door just enough to peer out. The woman I had mistaken
for Valerie was casually waiting for her bus and I almost col-
lapsed with relief. I remained in the bathroom until five minutes
before the bus was due for Newark Airport.

"Sir," I requested of a brawny fellow waiting in the depot,
"I'm sick and I can't lift my suitcase. Would you please help me
get it on the bus?" He pleasantly accommodated me and soon
I was on the bus bound for the airport.

I made my plane, with only minutes to spare. I was about
to become John Hughes. That was the name on my ticket, a
name I had carefully chosen for anonymity; it was also the name
of our family physician. All my previous terror seemed like
nothing when I saw none other than Dr. John Hughes standing in line for the same flight. I buried my face in a newspaper,
and kept my face down during the entire five-hour flight. I
removed neither my hat nor my sunglasses and I died a little
more each minute because I couldn't be sure whether Dr.
Hughes had recognized me or not.

I needn't have worried. My plot worked all too well. I'd hoped
that the authorities would assume I had drowned, but I was
stunned when I read in the papers that a body had actually
washed ashore the morning after I vanished. Not only that, it
was first spotted only a few feet from where I was last seen.
More astounding still, it fit my description, but divers were unable
to retrieve it before it was swept out to sea by a violent riptide.

Convinced that the corpse was the son of the grieving
Burkans, the police and clergy advised a memorial service to
recognize the loss. Three hundred people gathered for the sad
occasion. At the close of the ceremony, local politicians announced that because of the years I spent in volunteer service
to the community, a section of the new library was to be named
in my honor. A Memorial Library Fund was established and

Memorial Services
For Bruce Burkan

PARSIPPANY - The family of Bruce Burkan, who has been missing since Aug. 22, will hold memorial services for the 19-year old boy Sunday at 1 p. m.

Bruce, eldest son of Mr. and Mrs. Theodore Burkan of 400 Littleton Road, has been the object of an intensive air, sea and shoreline search since he left his fiancee, Valerie ꞏ ꞏ ꞏ ꞏ ꞏ ꞏ of ꞏ ꞏ ꞏ ꞏ ꞏ Road, on the beach at Asbury Park to put a coin in a parking meter. It is feared that a body seen in the surf two days later may have been Bruce's, although divers have failed to locate the body.

A nationwide hunt for the young man has turned up no clues as to his disappearance.

"We've accepted the fact of his death," said his mother.

"If our son were alive, he would come home. If he's wandering around somewhere, he would have been seen by now."

The services, conducted by Rabbi David Levy of Temple B'Nai Or and Dr. Norman Fletcher of the Unitarian Church of Montclair, will be held at the Temple, 330 South Street, Morristown. The service is not a private one.

A Bruce Burkan Library Memorial Fund, to benefit the Parsippany Library, has been established. Friends and relatives are asked to make donations to the Fund instead of sending flowers to the memorial service.

Donations should be sent to Mrs. Catherine Burns, Parsippany Library, 3199 Route 46, Parsippany. The money will be used to purchase books and equip a children's corner for young readers.

Bruce, a well-known area magician, had entertained children at St. Clare's and Riverside hospital pediatrics wards frequently.

"At Christmas," said Mrs. Burkan, "he visited the wards as a clown and gave the kids gifts which he'd purchased for them."

money was contributed from all over the country; people who had seen me perform read about my death and sent their contributions long after they had moved from New Jersey. I followed all these events in the newspapers from my rented room in a boardinghouse near Wilshire and Western in Los Angeles.

On the surface, everything went smoothly. In addition to forging documents that enabled me to change my name, I also created the necessary paperwork to change my age to twenty-one. I obtained credit cards, insurance, a new social security number and opened bank accounts. After the hemorrhaging stopped, which took about a week, I got a job selling shoes at Kinney's in Santa Monica, passed my California driver's test, bought a motorcycle and began commuting thirteen miles to work. Six weeks later, I was promoted to assistant manager. For all intents and purposes, I was on the road to a new and successful life as John Hughes.

At night, however, my guilt over the murder of my mother's son began eroding any pleasure I might have had in this new life. Fear and despair mounted daily so that soon I was in constant pain. I discovered in the act of living it that although I'd changed my name, my identity remained exactly the same. I dwelt on my psychotic behavior even more than I had before, condemning myself for running away, especially in the *way* I did. I was ashamed of myself; I hated myself. No aspect of my personality seemed redeeming. I began to suffer migraine headaches and severe stomach pains. My palms were wet and perspiration ran from my armpits in a never-ending stream. I had constant diarrhea. I was completely miserable.

I tried to examine my own mental condition, but objectivity was impossible. I imagined everything from latent homosexuality to suppressed homicidal tendencies. I fantasized murdering all the people I loved, blaming them for my emotional problems. Imagining such things made me even more disgusted with myself, and I soon convinced myself that I was hopelessly maladjusted, a damaged specimen of the species for whom there would be no peace of mind in this lifetime. I regretted not having killed myself in the first place instead of embarking on the demented scheme that only resulted in the illusion of my death.

With so much success in my life, I asked myself what possible explanation could there be for my emotional trauma? Obviously I was defective merchandise, best thrown into the crusher to be remade from scratch.

One morning, two and-a-half months after I had arrived in Los Angeles, I awoke in a cold sweat with my heart pounding wildly. My discomfort had grown to such a point that I was incapable of thinking coherently. Dressing in less than a minute, I ran from the house and into the flow of traffic. Horns sounded, brakes screeched and speeding vehicles swerved out of control in an effort to avoid squashing the crazy bug that had darted from nowhere into the busy street. Dazed, I stared blankly at the panicked drivers shaking their fists at me in justifiable anger. I made an obscene gesture at an overweight truck driver, turned and vanished into a throng of pedestrians. Sometime later I discovered myself at Los Angeles International Airport. Within an hour, leaving all my belongings behind, I was aboard a jet for New Jersey.

Two months had passed since my funeral, and my family and fiancée had resumed living their lives without me. My mother was still on tranquilizers, however, and needed sleeping pills to knock her out at night. My father still agonized over the fact that there was no body, no evidence to convince him of the finality of my fate. That created more torment for him than if I had been struck dead by lightning; the constant uncertainty prevented him from ever feeling at peace.

I later learned that during this time, a man phoned my parents to say he had read about what had happened to me, and that a red-haired boy about my age recently applied for a job in his store in New York City. He gave my parents the address the boy had put on the job application. It was in Mountain Lakes, New Jersey, only seven miles from my parents' home. My mother and father immediately drove there and knocked on the door of the large house that bore the address. The door was opened by a woman who instantly recognized my parents from their pictures in the newspapers. Sensing why they must have come, she burst into tears. An unspoken message passed among the three of them, and my parents also began to cry. The woman's nephew came to see what the noise was. He had red hair and was about my height and complexion. It was easy to see how a stranger might have mistaken him for me. But he was not my parents' son. They returned home in deeper grief than ever.

My grandfather, who had been enjoying his retirement until my disappearance, had forced himself to work long strenuous hours finishing my parents' basement to distract himself from his sorrow. It was he who bore the full brunt of the shock when I walked through the door of my parents' home. He was carrying a bag of groceries from the basement to the kitchen when suddenly the sight of his deceased grandson paralyzed his arms and caused the blood to leave his face. With his voice straining to escape his throat, he began screaming my mother's name over and over again. My mother, who was upstairs on the phone, called down to ask him what the matter was. "It's Bruce," he screamed. "Bruce is here! It's Bruce." My grandfather began to tremble and cry, falling to his knees.

My mother was immediately at the top of the stairs, phone in hand one moment, on the floor the next. She stood there in stunned disbelief, then, with a scream of "My God!" she flew from the top step to the bottom and clutched me in her arms, sobbing without control. By now my grandfather was embracing us both. For the next ten minutes, no one spoke a word; we sobbed, gasped for air, squeezed and kissed.

Emotions continued to run high that day as my brothers came home from school, my father came home from work, and finally, Valerie arrived. To my amazement, even though I told them the truth about why I had run away, these incredible human beings showed me the nature of real love. There was no anger, only gratitude that their deepest wish had come true: I was not dead. It was that day I realized for the first time how much my father really loved me. I didn't ask to be forgiven. Lost, confused, convinced beyond a doubt of my own insanity and overwhelmed by the unconditional love that allowed my family to accept me so totally, I placed myself completely in their hands, agreeing to do whatever they advised.

It was decided I should search for a psychiatrist who would be able to reach me. If the first wasn't right, there would be a second, if the second wasn't right, there would be a third. It was assumed that somewhere there was a doctor with the skill and compassion needed to help me. Valerie, too, had a plan to aid my recovery. Instead of rejecting me outright as I had anticipated, she suggested we marry immediately so that she could live by my side and help me along with her love and care. Engulfed by a sense of my own unworthiness to be shown such kindness, for three days I was able to do little more than lie in bed and weep.

In the midst of this, another powerful force played its own role in dealing with my return: the media. Someone recognized me en route to my parents' home and soon the yard was swarming with mobile television units, reporters and photographers. When reporters demanded an explanation for my apparent resurrection, we decided to say that I was suffering from amnesia and could remember nothing. Thus, there were no comments to give, no lengthy explanations, no justifications.

Of course, the media wasn't satisfied, and they plagued us for weeks. On the theory that some black and white snapshots of me would alleviate some of the pressure from reporters, I consented to a limited number of newspaper interviews and photo sessions. I didn't dare appear on television news or talk shows, however, for fear that if I were shown in color someone from California would recognize my red hair and undermine the amnesia story by revealing details of my assumed life there

FOR HOME DELIVERY

DAILY NEWS

NEW YORK'S PICTURE NEWSPAPER ®

CALL MU. 2-1234 COLLECT-EXT. 8156

Vol. 49. No. 106 Copr 1967 News Syndicate Co. Inc.   New York, N.Y. 10017, Thursday, October 26, 1967*   WEATHER: Cloudy, windy, cooler.

SON RETURNS AFTER HIS WAKE

'No one ever knows how much he will be mourned at his funeral. I've had the unique opportunity of returning. I never dreamed so many people cared about me.'

Bruce Burkan, 19, missing for two months and presumed dead, is reunited with his girl friend, Valerie ⸺ ⸺ in Parsippany, N. J. —*Story on page 3*   NEWS photo by Joe Petrella

Missing Son Back Home

—Associated Press Wirephoto

Bruce Burkan, 19, of Parsippany, N.J., had been missing and presumed dead for the past two months when he suddenly reappeared at his home and was given a welcoming kiss by his mother, Mrs. Theodore Burkan. He said he had no idea what had happened and couldn't remember where he had been.

as John Hughes. There would be no pretense of not having been conscious of making choices all along if it became known that I had emerged in Los Angeles complete with a forged birth certificate and clearly calculated new age.

My name was in headlines around the world. "Son Returns from the Grave" was a favorite story wired by press services everywhere. Friends sent me press clippings from Europe, Australia, even the Far East. Magazines were enthralled with reporting the news of the first magician in history to return from the dead. I offered no explanation for my disappearance, and the theories proposed by others grew more and more wild. One magazine reported that I had been kidnapped aboard a flying saucer and had my mind erased. Television and movie producers tried to buy the rights to "my story" for scripts they wanted to develop; religious leaders wrote for testimony that I had been resurrected; medical experts wanted to examine me to find the cause of my amnesia. I refused them all and quietly sought refuge in my parents' home. I felt crushed under the burden of publicity.

Two months later I was married. Three months after that, I saw someone housebreaking a dog, and I noticed that the old newspaper on which the dog sat bore headlines about an amnesic. The dog made a bull's-eye on my face. So much for fame and headlines, I thought to myself. How appropriate.

5

I was not in good shape. Although I had settled into a routine with a psychiatrist, and discussed with him the facts of my life, I didn't actually feel that things were improving. Once more — just as I had done before my disappearance — I hid the symptoms of my extreme discomfort. I wanted to do whatever I could to relieve the fears my family had for my well-being. And once more I was successful at my manipulation: my escape into "health" masked the fact that my inner condition really remained unchanged. My only reason for going to the psychiatrist was because it was expected of me.

Part of my healthy persona included a recommitment to my flourishing career. The massive amount of publicity generated by my return created such a demand for the Magic Clown show that I did not re-enroll in school. Soon I was booking shows not only here but abroad, commanding as much as five hundred dollars for half an hour. I performed for hotels, night clubs, corporations, organizations and private parties. My successful image was also supported by the expensive gifts I had taken to buying for Valerie — a mink coat and diamonds — and myself — a new car. Having these things didn't bring me joy, but they seemed to go along with the lifestyle I was adopting, and I had decided before the marriage that I was going to go all the way in trying to do what I considered to be "the right things."

But more often than not I felt that I was on the same well-oiled treadmill I had vowed to avoid — and I still couldn't see a reason for being on it, other than that it seemed to be the only path available. One thing that particularly confused me about my situation was that while all the other adults I knew, including my parents, seemed to work so hard for what they had, I put out so little and reaped so much. It seemed disproportionate. My success just underlined my confusion about myself and my place in the world. If I still wasn't happy with all that I had — and the prospect of having more didn't seem to promise any more happiness — what could I possibly do in order to be happy?

This question continued to play a central role in my secret mental life.

When I was twenty, about eigthteen months after Valerie and I were married, it occurred to me that by looking up my biological father, I might get some insight into the behavior patterns I found so diffucult to accept in myself. Since my mother told me she didn't know where to find him, I conducted a brief investigation. She had once mentioned having had to work during her first marriage because her husband was still in college, studying to be a teacher. So I began my search by phoning State Boards of Education in the northeast, plying the clerks with inquiries. I soon discovered that far from being the total incompetent I had imagined him to be, my birth father was a Ph.D. and principal of a school in Connecticut. I called him at his office one afternoon, and immediately lost my voice. On the other end of the phone I heard him saying "Hello? Hello? Hello?"

AGE TWENTY

When my voice finally squeaked, "Hello, this is Bruce Burkan," *he* was unable to speak. Now *I* was saying "Hello? Hello? Hello?"

After regaining his composure, he kept the conversation brief, inviting Valerie and me up to Connecticut that weekend to meet him, his wife and the three half-brothers I had never even known to exist — eleven-year-old Mitchell and the nine-year-old twins, Philip and Joey.

We had lunch and dinner together, looked at photo albums, began to get to know each other. By way of an explanation about his lack of communication with me, he said that after he had given me up for adoption, he had sought to contact me through my grandmother, and had been advised not to come between me and my new father. It was a wonderful visit for me, and I felt some resentment that so many secrets had been kept from me. Apparently, my mother really had known for some time where her former husband lived, that he had remarried, had three sons and had achieved a respected positon in his community. When I discovered this for myself, I envisioned my prospective relationship with my half-brothers and new family as a delightful additon to my life.

But it turned out to be hellish. My half-brothers had been even more in the dark about my existence than I had been about theirs; they hadn't even known that their father had been married before. When we finally met, the strain on their family resulting from my sudden appearance in their lives eventually caused my father to discontinue all contact with me, but not before I was involved enough to feel I was being rejected totally.

My parents were relieved when I stopped seeing my biological father's family. The prospect that his family might have become important to me had hurt them. Now that was at least one aspect of my life they didn't have to worry about. From my perspective, it was just one more in a long series of disappointments. Even the fact that my biological father wasn't the madman I had at times feared him to be paled in comparison to the hurt I felt from his unwillingness to build a relationship with me.

Around this time another factor added to my instability. Although I maintained complete fidelity to Valerie, I became more and more involved in sexual fantasies that began to evaporate my previous desire for monogamy. I often felt a burning desire to have sexual intercourse with anyone I was socially attracted to. I still believed I should be monogamous, however, and, as a consequence, rather than producing any pleasure, these fantasies served only to increase the level of my inner stress. My method of coping was exactly as it had always been: I continued being a master at suppressing and disguising what I regarded as the symptoms of my gross mental illness, which meant that my entire life was an act of deception — just as it had been before I disappeared.

The strain of my self-control made me like a pressure cooker, and my treatment with the psychiatrist was doing nothing to reduce the pressure. As far as I was concerned, he was just another character to be manipulated in my melodrama. Having no confidence in his ability to help me, I gave him no opportunity to try. I spoke to him about everything — except my utter contempt for him and his profession.

6

Three years slowly passed after I returned from the dead and my worst fears were being realized: everything was continuing to be the same. I was acquiring more success, more renown as a performer. I was traveling more and purchasing more. But regardless of how many acquisitions in the way of things and experiences I was adding to my life, "something" was still missing. I still never felt fulfilled, never felt happy. In fact, after three years of watching my condition, I was utterly miserable. Despair over not finding a way out of my predicament brought out the idea of suicide more strongly than ever before.

I let my mind dwell on thoughts of death for months while also trying to figure out other solutions to relieve my constant stress. Valerie and I were on a two-week cruise in the Caribbean aboard the S. S. Leonardo Da Vinci when I finally decided that I wanted a divorce. I broke down and cried, telling her everything that I thought was wrong with me, concluding that there was not enough in life to nourish me or make me want more. I told her, with shame, that I even fantisized converting my skills of deception into a life of professional crime because at least it would be more exciting than our prosaic lifestyle.

The fact that I permitted these fantasies into my mind reviled me to myself even more. I felt I had to be perfect in word, thought and deed just to have the right to exist. Imperfect as I was, I felt unworthiness and depression beyond description, and I could no longer live with the constant stress of trying to be the man whom I felt Valerie should have married, a man I felt I would never be.

I told Valerie she could keep all our money and material possessions and I would "live in the woods." I had learned excellent camping skills as an Eagle Scout and thoughts of living in the forest seemed to dominate my mind as the only possibility for hope. I finally admitted to Valerie that I hadn't made any progress with the psychiatrist and that I *often* felt like killing myself. I explained that since I couldn't see any reason for my melancholia, I must be defective, maybe even brain-damaged.

Valerie was crushed. She had a wellspring of compassion for me in addition to her own sorrow and grief. We discussed and discussed, we cried, we hugged, but we both sensed the inevitable: that even though our parting would create a loss for both of us, I needed to escape from "something" and she would soon be living alone. We decided to remain together two more weeks to explore any possible alternatives that might occur to us. Since our outer lives seemed so glamorous and buoyant, I dreaded the thought of how shocked and disappointed our families would be. I particularly dreaded seeing Valerie's father, Paul, who had remained so close to me, even after I had run away, and who was going to meet our ship when we docked in New York.

But, when we finally reached New York, Paul wasn't there. With a sense of foreboding, Valerie and I returned home by bus and Valerie immediately began calling family and friends to find out about her father. No one answered until she called her Uncle Otto, Paul's brother. Otto began weeping on the phone and would only say that Paul was in the hospital.

That afternoon, we visited him. Paul had cancer of the nervous system. It was inoperable. Two weeks later, Valerie's brother, Teddy, married his girlfriend, Linda; several days after that, Paul was dead. Only after he died did Valerie and I finally start living apart and planning a divorce. Our separation did nothing to improve my spirits. I still hated life; I felt as if I were the last remaining piece of a huge jigsaw puzzle that had been arduously assembled, but though only one space remained unfilled, I didn't fit into it.

In the autumn of 1970, during the first two months of my separation from Valerie, my brother, Barry, phoned me at the rooming house where I was living in Verona, New Jersey, and told me, "Grandma has cancer." I barely heard him say that it was operable and that doctors were "optimistic," I was so overcome by a sense of loss that all I could do was burst into tears. The conversation didn't end there, however. I soon learned that Valerie's mother, Dolores, was also in the hospital. There were some problems with her vision and it was suspected that she had a brain tumor. Neither she nor Grandma knew that the other was in the same hospital on the same floor, just several rooms away. I was told not to mention Grandma's hospitalization to Valerie's mother if I called her and not to mention Dolores's hospitalization if I called Grandma.

When I hung up the phone, all the guilt I was carrying from leaving Valerie and from running away three years before surged through me, breaking down the last vestige of resistance I had to killing myself. For years I had felt so black inside and had not wanted to burden the ones I loved by sharing this blackness with them, but obviously I had not been able to prevent them from being affected by it. I felt *I* was the cancer in their lives and that if I destroyed myself in one final flourish, in time they would be able to recover. Locking the door of my rented room, I downed enough sleeping pills to kill five men.

I remember nothing of my initial hospitalization. The doctors told my parents I couldn't possibly survive. At one point, my heart stopped. Although the medical experts succeeded in not losing me at that moment, they told my parents it would only be a matter of hours until I would be dead.

I survived the week-long coma, however, and was moved from the intensive care unit to a semi-private room in the same hospital as Grandma and Dolores. Valerie and my parents would visit my room where I lay unconscious, then don their coats and go to Dolores's room, then, after visiting her, again put on their coats as if they were leaving the hospital and go instead to Grandma's room. Even those who retained their health were in torture at this point.

But for me, although I didn't know it, the torture was just beginning.

As soon as my doctors felt I was strong enough, I was sent directly from the hospital to a private mental institution. It was considered a posh retreat, catering to the elite, but there were still bars on the windows, and patients were not allowed to have matches, razors or belts. Once there, I was put on heavy doses of tranquilizers, given a battery of in-depth psychological tests and treated with psychotherapy. I was soon diagnosed as schizophrenic and was scheduled for electric shock treatments. After several weeks of electric shock, deep insulin coma therapy was initiated to further remove the peaks and valleys from my personality, and hopefully, with them, any remaining desire I might have to kill myself.

Every morning I was to be awakened at 4:00 a.m. and strapped to a table. A massive overdose of insulin would then be injected so that moments later I would be comatose.

The first day it began, I was jostled from sleep and, still a bit disoriented, I was led downstairs along tiled corridors while a succession of doors were unlocked for my entry, then bolted behind me. The treatment room was sterile and laboratory-like, divided by a flimsy curtain on one side of which lay the women and on the other, the men. We were seven altogether.

Several days of testing were required to determine exactly how much insulin was needed to put me in a deep coma. The first morning I didn't succumb completely, and so, half-awake, I watched the procedure consume the patients around me who had already been in the routine for weeks.

As I lay there strapped to the table I heard a woman scream from behind the curtain. Before I could even react, the man on the table next to me began shuddering and vibrating the platform to which he was tied. I looked over and saw his mouth twisted and foaming, his eyes rolled up in their sockets, leaving only the whites. Moments later, in a spasm, his elimination system went out of control, and he soiled his treatment gown with his own excrement. Guttural sounds gurgled from his throat and joined with the sobs, screams and moans of the other patients.

I knew that I would enter the ranks of those surrounding me as soon as the exact measure of insulin needed to send me over the threshold had been reached. Horrified, all I could think of during those first hours was how I could successfully kill myself before my turn came to join the "coma club," but the institution had, of course, been made suicide-proof.

Each morning I was injected with a larger dose until, on the third morning, the insulin finally won me over and I was plunged into terror. My mouth seemed to be filled with cotton, and when I pleaded for water, I was told, "No!"

"Please," I begged.

"No!"

"Please, I can't even swallow. . . just a sip?"

"No!"

The air seemed to buzz with a strange sound and the shape of objects in the room constantly changed. One moment the orderly in charge was human and, in the next, as the insulin began to take effect, he was a monstrous demon whose very presence made my skin hot with fear. Unseen dogs barked from beneath the treatment table and my body writhed in its harness.

My tongue felt as if it was sliding down my throat and I began to choke. But I had little time for concern. Suddenly my head exploded and splattered my brain all over the tiled white walls and whitewashed ceiling. Now everything was black and I swirled away into infinite space becoming nothing more than dizziness and pain.

At about noon, an antidote known as glucagon was administered and I awoke from the coma.

This continued for three months, at which point the doctors told my parents I was "cured" and sent me home.

Looking back, I can see that I started on the road that led to my second suicide attempt in the spring of 1971, the exact moment I was being released from the mental hospital. I was overweight from the high sugar diet I had been forced to consume in conjunction with the insulin coma treatments, and I was still taking heavy sedatives. I resembled a zombie. I had no complaints: I was numb, dazed, and completely flattened. I had the personality of a marshmallow and slept most of the day. The cure was a curse.

And as if the serpent's tooth hadn't bitten deep enough, ten months after Paul died, when I got out of the mental hospital, Valeries' brother, Teddy, my best friend, was killed in a head-on car collision. He died instantly and his wife, Linda, who was eight months pregnant, lost the baby and was in critical condition. The pain of Paul's and Teddy's deaths was so intense for me I dared not let myself feel it; I started using the sedating drugs in larger and larger doses so that I would experience as little as possible of any feeling.

Grandma seemed to be recovering from her surgery and the prognosis was still good. Dolores underwent brain surgery and the tumor that had been blurring her vision was successfully removed. Her recovery was rapid and promising. My reality was spinning, changing, whirling so fast that I lived on the edge of constant dizziness for months.

Everyone involved was coping in his or her own way. Valerie, whose burden was the greatest, counseled with a therapist; Dolores eventually returned to work; Grandma and Grandpa took a vaction in Florida, and my parents went about running their real estate and insurance business.

Several months after my discharge from the hospital, a friend who was a cruise director compassionately offered to let me come aboard ship as his assistant. Implicit in his suggestion was the idea that life aboard a luxury liner at sea is as sedating as any drug or institution. Indeed, upon coming aboard I had stewards and maids attending to all my needs from food preparation and laundry to shoe shines and making my bed. In this environment, away from home and family, I gradually stopped using the Thorazine and other drugs, and my personality again began to take on some color.

The two years between my first attempt to kill myself and Taylor Caldwell's party on the Rotterdam were years of travel. Twelve months passed during which I spent only twenty-two days in America. One of those twenty-two days I spent in court, legally dissolving my marriage. At that point I held the proverbial clean slate in my hands and could have written anything on it that would start my life anew.

But what did I do?

Without any new discoveries on my part, I proceeded to redo the same old scenes I had played throughout my life — and this was despite the fact that during this time I had a meeting with a most remarkable woman who, had I really been able to hear her in my heart, provided me with all the information I needed to find the happiness for which I so vainly searched.

7

Almost a year before Taylor Caldwell's party, in the spring
of 1972, while docked in New York, I confided to my brother,
Barry, that I still felt suicidal. Barry responded by taking me to
meet his meditation teacher, Hilda Charlton.

I was brought to an incense-filled apartment on the sixth floor
of a building on the Upper West Side. The walls were filled with
pictures of the world's most famous saints: Jesus, Buddah,
Krishna. Perhaps a dozen people, conspicuous in their devotion to Hilda, sat cross-legged on the carpet. As I took my seat
among them, I was surprised to find myself — who had only
vaguely heard of meditation and certainly didn't practice it —
actually comfortable there.

Hilda struck me as very old. I thought she must have been
in her seventies at the time, although now I know she couldn't
have been nearly that old. She was wearing a silk sari and had
dyed red-brown hair. I found it funny that she could be a spiritual
woman and still have dyed hair. But what struck me most profoundly was that despite her age, there was a vitality to her,

HILDA CHARLTON

the kind of special life-force, strength and enthusiasm usually seen only in children. In her deep-set eyes there was infinite wisdom. I had never seen such eyes: they were clear grey-blue, penetrating yet kind.

Without question, she was a presence to be reckoned with, and when she spoke, chatty though she appeared, her voice held the power of utmost authority. "Why would you consider killing yourself?" she asked with a laugh.

"Because I'm so miserable that I'm actually in pain," I replied.

"Where's the pain? Is it in your legs? Is it in your arms? Perhaps the pain is in your chest? Could I find it using a stethoscope? Are you having headaches? Is it in your head?"

I thought Hilda was ridiculing me.

Suddenly she almost shouted, "Dummy! Can't you see the pain isn't in your body? You could very well succeed in killing your body and *you* would still be miserable. Wait until you're happy, *then* kill yourself!" She laughed irreverently.

A rush of insight flooded my mind. By Hilda's grace I felt as if I had suddenly seen LIGHT. Although I didn't know exactly what I had seen, and had no idea how to express it, nevertheless I felt I had glimpsed the flickerings of a new truth, a new philosophy. And sensing this new truth that I couldn't put into words, life no longer seemed hopeless to me. I suddenly felt there were things I really did not know, lessons I had not learned, no matter how well I had done in school or how accomplished I was as a magician. There were people like Hilda, I now realized, who had answers to questions I had never even thought of asking.

My brain shook with excitement. Sitting in front of this ageless old woman named Hilda, I felt ready to explore another reality, a reality that promised to give added dimension and meaning to the one I had always assumed to be the *only* reality. Hilda herself was clearly in touch with a reality much larger than my limited concepts; it was part of what created her special energy and humor. She didn't seem to be locked into the same behaviors and emotions as everyone else I knew; she seemed to have an ability to see and hear things that other people, including myself, couldn't see and hear.

I didn't just treat Hilda as if I was showing respect to an older person; I was in awe. All at once I realized that the magic I was practicing was a mere counterfeit of something else — that there was such a thing as *real* magic. This was the kind of magic I wanted in my future!

The problem I faced now was how to find it.

After the time she spent focusing on me in the supportive atmosphere provided by her students, Hilda was by no means through with the help she was offering. She reached for the phone, dialed a number, and immediately began a conversation which we could all overhear.

"Hello, Ram Dass," she said. "I have someone here I'd like you to talk with, may I send him over? . . . Fine, he'll be there shortly."

Barry was handed an address and instructed to bring me to see this person whom Hilda was calling Ram Dass. Although all of this was done very matter-of-factly, I experienced it as an exciting adventure, and I wondered what would happen next. A short taxi ride brought the answer.

Ram Dass turned out to be a woolly fellow in his forties with blue eyes, a bushy beard and Levi jeans. He greeted us with a hug and led us to a small room where we sat on the floor and sipped tea. Presently, Barry was asked to make himself comfortable in another room, and Ram Dass sat facing me alone.

RAM DASS

I was impressed by his gentleness and the sense of inner peace that revealed itself in his eyes. He had a calming effect on me, and soon I was telling him of my past, dwelling on the ugliest aspects of my behavior — the ones that were ever-present on my mind.

"You're really open," he twinkled. "You're really beautiful."

"Hmmmmm," I pondered, "he's not seeing 'my psychoses.'"

I did everything I could to reveal my defective personality, but the blacker I tried to paint myself, the more he would laugh and say, "You're beautiful, you're so beautiful."

"He's not getting it," I thought again. With embellishments, I outlined for him the events of my funeral, my suicide attempt, and other events in my life that I felt illustrated my reprehensible misconduct and my reason for walking around in a perpetual cloud of guilt.

"It's all melodrama," he said, with ultimate composure. "True, as melodramas go, you win a prize, but it's still just melodrama. Everybody has a melodrama. And behind all THAT! *here we are.*"

Though I couldn't feel these new concepts deep in my gut, or explain what I was so dimly beginning to understand, Ram Dass's words gave me another flickering glimpse into the reality of which Hilda had spoken, a reality not of the body, not of the world I knew, the world with which I was so dissatisfied, filled with all its "symbols" of success. When I told Ram Dass about how difficult it was for me living life in current society, he told me a story about a tailor named Zumbach.

It seems that Zumbach was world-renowned for the fine-fitting clothes he created. His prices were the highest anywhere and he had a long waiting list of people desiring his services. A common man of ordinary means one day decided that he would save all his money until he could finally afford to purchase one of Zumbach's tailor-made suits for himself.

The man saved and saved until at last he had enough money. He visited Zumbach several times for the necessary fittings. When the custom suit was ready, he received a call from Zumbach telling him to come pick up his new clothes. The man was very excited, but when he put the suit on and stood in front of the mirror, he immediately noticed that one sleeve was longer than the other. "Zumbach," he said, "one sleeve is too short."

"Oh, no, no," Zumbach reassured him, "You're standing wrong. Raise your shoulder and stand like this."

The man contorted his body in an exact imitation of the way Zumbach had contorted his, and sure enough, the sleeves looked fine.

Ram Dass moved his shoulders around to illustrate the story he was telling, then he continued.

"Zumbach," the man cried, looking at his reflection in the mirror, "What you said was true, but when I stand this way the collar bunches up and won't fit around my neck properly."

Zumbach calmly replied, "You're still not standing properly. Hunch a bit like this and shift your position like so."

Imitating the new stance which the tailor demonstrated, the man looked in the mirror and discovered that now the collar fell perfectly. At this point, however, he noticed that despite all his contortions the buttons did not seem to line up as they should.

Zumbach then instructed the man to deform himself even more and, pointing at the mirror, he proudly exclaimed, "Look, a perfect fit!"

So the man left the tailor wearing his new suit. His body is scrunched into a strange position and he hobbles to a bus stop to await the downtown local. While standing there, a passing pedestrian admiringly exclaimed, "What a gorgeous suit! It must be a Zumbach suit. Am I right?"

"Yes, yes, it is a Zumbach suit," the man said, proud to be wearing such a mark of distinction. "How could you tell?"

The stranger replied, "Well, sir, only a tailor as fine as Zumbach could so perfectly fit a cripple like you."

"You're like the man wearing Zumbach's suit," Ram Dass told me. "You've twisted yourself to the point of agony trying to squirm into a suit you were never meant to wear. Be yourself. Don't let society or anyone dictate to you how you must be. Just be who you are . . . You're beautiful. Remove all restraints on your inner feelings. Don't limit yourself or what you are willing to experience. And in the middle of letting yourself expand, step back and note, 'Behind all *THAT*, here *we* are.' Love yourself for doing whatever you do. You are a perfect expression of God."

A perfect expression of God?

I felt so totally imperfect — and had felt that way for so long — it never even occurred to me that I could accept myself just as I was. It was a completely new idea to think of myself as perfect — perfect despite the fact that I had anger and pain inside me, perfect even when I was hating those dearest to me, perfect even when I was so ashamed of my human emotions that I felt I couldn't live with them — perfect even when I had tried to do away with myself.

Suddenly being alive was revealing its perfection to me.

As Ram Dass said goodbye to us with a hug, he invited me to visit him whenever I was in port. I was impressed to realize that neither he nor Hilda had taken any money for the service they had given me, nor had they once looked at their watches. Five days later, Barry gave me a copy of Ram Dass's book, *Be Here Now,* in which he recounted the story of his pioneering self-transformation through LSD and his conversion to Eastern mysticism. I was astonished to discover that the man who had been so humble and generous with me was a world-renowned celebrity and teacher. I was very moved by how special were these new people in my life.

I never would have believed then that one year later I would be recovering from a second attempt at suicide, this time not as the impassioned response to an upsetting phone call, but because many hours of deep reflection would convince me that it was a "logical" next step.

9

In the weeks following my initial meetings with Hilda and Ram Dass, I bought scores of books on the subjects of mysticism and Eastern philosophy. Barry told me that Hilda had lived in India for nineteen years and studied with some of the world's greatest spiritual teachers, men with names I had never heard before: Nityananda, Mahatabananda, Sai Baba. Barry also described healings people had received in India and miraculous acts that had been observed there, like walking on fire, levitating, and materializing and dematerializing objects. I decided I would have to make a pilgrimage there, so that I would be touched by this magic. I knew, however, that such a pilgrimage lay several months ahead of me, when I could take time off from my work aboard ship. For the present, I contented myself with reading the Masters' printed words in the volumes I now carried with me wherever I went.

The books on Buddhism cited "attachment" as the root cause of all suffering, so in grand acts of generosity I began to divest myself of the wealth I had accumulated. My high-mindedness was not always appropriate, however, or even appreciated; I gave to strangers gifts so valuable that the recipients seemed more frightened than pleased to receive them. I met a young woman in Denmark and, playing my version of Prince Charming, whisked her into my court aboard ship, waltzed her around the world for a few turns, delighting myself with how much I could bestow on my "Cinderella."

As I traveled, I purchased gifts for everyone I knew. Not a possession nor a penny did I wish to keep. I was drunk and delirious with what I thought was happiness, but of course it wasn't. If I had missed the point of the philosophy I was studying, at least I was enjoying myself, perhaps for the first time since my mid-teens. I thought I was on the path to "enlightenment" — I knew certainly I was seeking it — but the truth was, I couldn't even have recognized enlightenment. I was still mad, I was just expressing it differently. The books I was reading intoxicated me and I danced about not in mystical bliss, but in a state of mystification. In the midst of this foolishness, my grandmother, whom I adored more than any other being on the planet, died. Suddenly I was sober.

So quickly did I fall from ecstacy into despair that I doubted everything I had read and studied. Of what value was a *Nirvana* that could so easily evaporate? I was again stymied by confusion; all the teaching I had been trying to follow had still not begun to travel from my head to my heart.

Shortly after Grandma's death I visited Hilda in New York. She told me that in India there was a guru who always laughed and said "How wonderful!" when he was informed about a person's death. "Once you understand what God really is, Bruce," Hilda instructed, "you understand that a person's passing is cause for a celebration. It's their marriage to their beloved."

But I didn't understand, and I frequently felt morose. Soon I was visited by a dream.

A young woman was hitchhiking on the ramp of a freeway entrance. She was promiscuous, frequently sleeping with the men who gave her rides. One day she realized that months had passed since she had last menstruated. She was pregnant. Not knowing how she would deal with this, she simply decided to put it out of her mind for the present and continue to travel about. One day, however, she discovered herself going into labor. Quite calmly, she walked from the freeway ramp where she had been standing with her thumb extended and went into a nearby woods.

Squatting, she delivered her baby. It was an easy birth and she broke the cord with her teeth. For a few minutes the baby lay in the leaves, healthy, alive and crying. The girl suddenly and without emotion placed her hands around the baby's throat and choked the child until he was dead. She then covered the tiny corpse with bark, leaves and brush, cleaned herself and walked back to the freeway. She extended her thumb, hailed a car and hitchhiked away.

I awoke from the dream in a sweat, agitated, upset and bewildered. I very much identified myself with the baby, but couldn't make total sense of the dream. Several days passed, and I remained disturbed by the power of the dream. Then a rather ordinary thing happened that catalyzed a sequence of thoughts in my mind. I happened to be looking at a book of matches lying on a table when I closed my eye to rub out some dust. When I opened that eye, I closed the other eye so that I could rub it as well. The book of matches seemed to move, just slightly shifting its position on the table.

I glanced around the room, successively closing one eye, then the other. Everything in the room could be made to dance a bit as each eye closed and exposed a different perspective. My mind began to play with the notion of "Which is the real image?" My right eye created one matchbook, my left eye created another. Although the matchbooks were similar, nonetheless there was a definite difference between what each eye perceived.

It occurred to me that if someone else entered the room, he or she would perceive a completely different matchbook from either of the two that I observed. In fact, if the room were filled with flying insects, there would be thousands of matchbooks, as many thousands as there were eyes to see them. Although rationally I understood there was only one matchbook, a part of my mind was insisting that there would be as many matchbooks as there were observers, that the matchbook was literally being created by being perceived. And again I wondered, only now from the vantage point of almost an infinite number of matchbooks, which would be the "real" matchbook?

I began to have a strange premonition that the matchbook couldn't exist without me, that I was *actually* creating it. Suddenly the memory of my dream presented itself and in a flash I saw one dimension of its meaning, a dimension that once again flooded my mind with insight. Up until that moment, I had thought that the planet Earth had existed for perhaps three billion years and that I was only a temporary visitor, here for seventy years or so and then gone. I assumed the earth and "reality" as I knew it preceded me and would continue much the same after I was gone; now I was overwhelmed by the notion that I had been misunderstanding something pivotal all my life. Clearly, *the earth as I experienced it wasn't here for billions of years, it began with my birthday!* The reality that surrounds me and in which I thought I was immersed is only temporary, here for seventy years or so. When I depart, I take it all with me. The baby in the dream didn't live for a few minutes; the entire universe that child represented came and went in those minutes. On another level, the level "behind all *THAT*," as Ram Dass had called it, the baby had always existed and would continue to exist.

I suddenly felt that I had never been born and could never die, that I existed always and would continue forever. The Universe is eternal; only each particular universe is temporary, and there are as many universes as there are beings to create them. Furthermore, I realized, since each universe is slightly different, just like the matchbook viewed from different eyes, it is foolish to presume to know someone else's reality.

My mind had never thought along lines quite like this before, and my head was throbbing. "Which is the *real* matchbook?" I was determined to know. "What is *reality* anyway? One day I'm jubilant and the next I'm depressed; which is the *real* me?"

I mused to myself that if I asked someone to show me his car and all he brought me was the fender, I would have to say, "No, that's not the car, bring me your car." If he returned with a tire, again I would have to say, "No, that's not the car either." Soon I would have a whole pile of parts in front of me: carburetor, clutch, seats, chrome, dials, but still no car. "Where does the *real* car exist?" It doesn't, I concluded; the *real* car is a concept. Somehow, the whole is *greater* than the sum of its parts.

The next day I continued my inquiry into the nature of reality by going to the library and borrowing several books about Albert Einstein and his theory of relativity. Like a vacuum cleaner, my mind was sucking me into myself with questions, riddles and paradoxes. Two weeks later, I left for India.

I had one objective and one objective only in making this trip: I wanted finally to find "enlightenment." Since, as far as I knew, I had never met anyone who possessed this coveted quality, I admitted to myself that I really still didn't know what it was. Intuitively I felt it was that very essence of life that had always evaded me — the missing ingredient upon which my happiness depended. My troubled mind desperately needed evidence that enlightenment existed as an attainable possibility for earnest seekers. To me it represented life's ultimate secret. If I could attain it myself, I felt I would finally understand the nature of God, which was still totally unknown to me.

I had thought about God since childhood, but had had no real experience of Him through my perfunctory religious training for my Bar Mitzvah or afterwards. Being only a vague concept to me, I never turned to God in my need. The more I read about spiritual matters, however, the more I wanted to experience God as a reality. I looked at India as my last hope to accomplish this, and in planning the journey I scintillated with excitement about meeting the masters of life's real magic, the gurus who would transmute my experience of myself into that of a constantly glowing being.

In February, 1973, shortly after I arrived in India, I heard rumors that there was a man not far from Bombay who possessed all the qualities of God. It was reported that he performed miracles and personified the enlightenment I sought. He was definitely a "Master," as holy men of the highest development are called in the East. Rumor had it that he had the power to grant wishes and fulfill secret yearnings if the seeker was of pure heart. I learned that this God-man's name was Muktananda, which means "one who lives in freedom and bliss."

Bombay was beastly hot. The trip to the place I was told I would find Muktananda required connections between several buses and trains. But before journeying into the suburbs of Bombay, I decided to pursue another rumor. I was told that in the heart of the city itself dwelt Mahatabananda, one of the men with whom Hilda had studied. He was 171 years old, I heard, yet still retained the physical qualities of a man not yet sixty. Since I felt compelled on my pilgrimage to uncover each secret and mystery, despite the brutalizing heat and the overwhelming stench of a land so poor that people lived and died on the streets, I resolved to seek the ancient yogi who possessed knowledge of perpetual youth.

Navigation through the alien city was torture, but I was determined. The crush of people was awesome. Maimed babies wailed on doorsteps; lepers plagued every tourist for a rupee. Lepers! I was mortified; how could *I* be surrounded by lepers? Somehow I eventually arrived at the address I sought. Without hesitation, I pounded the portal that stood between me and the object of my traumatic search. A pleasant Indian fellow of approximately the same age as myself opened the door and inquired about the purpose of my visit. When I told him, he said simply, "Oh, I am so sorry, Yogi has just left his body only days ago."

"Left his body?" I asked incredulously. "You mean he's *dead.*"

"Yes," came the reply.

"Is it true he was 171 years old?" I asked.

"Oh, yes, yes, very true. With all his teeth. Yogi was a Master soul," the young man said.

I was momentarily inclined to ask if I could come in to speak at length with the fellow, since I had come with so many questions, but after brief consideration, instead I apologized for my intrusion and left. After all, I hadn't come all the way to India to chat about what may have very well been a myth. Since I still had my childhood habit of taking everything that happened on earth extremely personally, I actually became indignant that Mahatabananda would do this to me, and it undermined my belief in his powers. If he had been as great as I had heard, why didn't he wait to see me before he died? The discomfort of enduring the intense heat and foul odors was nothing compared to the ache of my disappointment.

As soon as I could, I boarded the train that would take me to Muktananda. Feces, vomit and urine filled the car with a disgusting smell. I tried to escape into the book I had brought, an explanation of Einstein's theory of relativity for the layman. What impressed me deeply was Einstein saying that he had received his insights by making a "leap of the imagination." Although I always had had a vivid imagination, I had considered imagination to be a limited tool. After discovering metaphysics, however, imagination began to take on a new scope for me. Reading about Einstein, I was delighted to discover his own respect for the ability of imagination to go beyond the beyond, even more powerfully than "warp drive" or a jump into "hyper space," since imagination requires no movement at all. Einstein's "leap," as I understood it, was simply a matter of "being there."

The more I read about physics the more my reality became

metaphysical. I was no longer seeing things as divided into two categories, energy and matter. I was becoming convinced that matter did not exist in the way I thought it did; there was only energy in different densities and forms. Every atom was a bundle of energy, that was all. Many of these atoms taken together may resemble a solid object, but they are still just energy, moving at a very slow speed. The mushroom cloud over Hiroshima became a dark reminder to me that the energy contained in a small bundle of "matter" can reorganize with such force that it can destroy an entire city in the process.

I began to feel intuitively that everything was connected, that each thing that appeared to be different only did so because it was of a different density of some all-pervasive, unifying energy. I could no longer regard matter as a "solid" island in an ocean of energy, for it was the *same* as the energy that surrounded it, like icebergs floating in the Arctic Sea.

This suggested a further implication to me: since we as human beings know for a fact that we possess intelligence, it seems that the energy field of which we are all a part must be intelligent as well. Although each individual in a dream has an existence separate from each of the other characters in the dream, no one in a dream exists outside the mind of the dreamer. The characters' "reality" is relative to the mind of the dreamer; none of the characters is created or destroyed; none is born, none dies; all are simply projected by and absorbed within one mind. Using this as an analogy for human existence, I began to think of my mind and the minds of everyone I knew as individual minds and also as existing within the Mind of God.

With these new concepts, metaphysics unveiled a Oneness for me that embraced everything. For the first time I could understand how in laboratory experiments in America, Russia and China, people were able to move objects without touching them (before I had thought all such people used tricks from magic catalogues) and how instances of telepathy were as real and logical as any consequence of the law of gravity (before I had always thought of them as mere coincidences).

All that I demanded from my trip to India was total proof that metaphysical phenomena were as real as I now imagined them to be. I also wanted to meet someone who understood the laws behind these phenomena and would be able to show me how they could be put to use. I was certain that would enable me to create a balanced and harmonious existence for myself. Once these laws were proven to me beyond a shadow of a doubt and I knew how to use them, then I was sure I would have integrated all the concepts I was learning.

I sensed that the renowned Swami Muktananda held the key to my ultimate happiness.

I arrived at his gate exhausted but enthusiastic and receptive. Tired of ministers, rabbis and priests who taught the mysteries of existence as a mundane subject with no more excitement than algebra, and unmoved by professors whose knowledge of life seemed to have come from textbooks, I was anxious to meet a man who really understood these esoteric principles of reality. I needed to see with my own eyes a human being who had grasped the nature of life and used this knowledge as the basis of his daily routine. I had no way of knowing what Swami Muktananda would be like, but I was hoping to encounter a radiant, joyous being who exuded an aura of ultimate compassion and understanding, knowing all the answers, wielding all the power of God, commanding all the energy available to the *One*.

The Muktananda I met that day was not at all the Wizard of Oz I had expected him to be. To my eyes, he looked like a sickly old man with wrinkled flesh, crumpled on a straw mat, barking irate commands at devoted followers who seemed ecstatic with his every croak. He couldn't even speak English; I was stunned. Surely the all-knowing one should be able to speak English! I thought.

Exhausted and proud — these were the adjectives I used in my mind to describe this holy man who touched millions of people all over the world, opening them to God realization. The fact that he didn't live up to *my* picture of who I wanted him to be disenchanted me totally and clouded all the sparkle that others perceived in him. Indeed, it appeared to me that the only power he had was given to him by the devotion and purity of his followers.

AGE TWENTY-FIVE

I somehow survived the trek back to Bombay and left India bitter and sad. My disappointment extinguished the light my hope had kindled. Returning to my life aboard ship, though I giggled and danced as I performed the antics of Tolly the Clown Magician, my heart was numb and my spirit crushed. Where was there left to go? At Taylor Caldwell's party I was deeply struck by the realization that I wasn't alone in my feelings of being lost and alienated; beneath their affluence and prestige, and despite the experience of age, it seemed that many of the guests were as lost as I was, and no more contented with "symbols" of success.

I had searched around the world trying to discover even one human being who embodied the enlightenment I had believed to exist. Even the thought of Hilda and Ram Dass seemed to depress me. It was all well and good for them to see so much beauty in life, but how was *I* going to reach that state of perception? Quite clearly, the answer was that I wouldn't. I was tired, confused and so strangled by doubt that all I wanted to do was sleep, to melt the iceberg of my life into a metaphysical sea. That was when I locked my cabin door and went to sleep for what I thought was the last time.

Instead of the return to Oneness that I had hoped would be mine, I found myself a cripple in bed, the victim of a second botched attempt at suicide, trying to make sense of who I was and what I was to do now that life had again played such a seemingly cruel trick on me by forcing me to continue with it. How was I to act around my parents, those poor frustrated souls who loved me so? How could I face Hilda who so optimistically set me on the path of discovery? What was the lesson in my being alive? Why was I being punished and for what crime?

My only answers came in the form of tears and I cried for days.

I had no idea if I would ever recover the use of my legs. They oozed syrupy fluids from decubitus ulcers at the pit of which lay exposed bone. These holes caused me no pain, however, because my legs were paralyzed and free from all feeling.

Several days after I had returned to my parents' home, Barry came up to my bedside late one night and told me he had been in New York where Hilda was conducting prayer sessions for my full recovery. He entreated me to see her, but even as he said the words, he could see I was in no condition to be moved.

I had attacked my body in early April, and, to my surprise, I was able to hobble on crutches by mid-May. Hilda was relentless in her prayer treatments and in June, with only a cane, I finally went to see her in Manhattan. The ugly sores were not yet completely healed and portions of each leg were still insensitive to touch or pain, but there was no doubt that mending was in progress.

Hilda shook her head as I hobbled through the door. She asked about my trip to India and I complained that there had been no miracles. She laughed. "Dummy! You still haven't learned a thing!" I avoided her knowing, compassionate eyes and stared at the floor. "Look at me!" she snapped. I complied instantly. Her eyes penetrated to the core of my being. "You're looking for miracles, eh? Why don't you look in the mirror? Your life is a miracle. You should be dead. Every law of science says so. But you're here. And look at your legs —"

I interrupted, sarcasm ringing in my voice, "Yeah, look at them."

"Ingrate!" she bellowed. "We've been working day and night healing those legs, and they *will* be healed. You want a miracle? You're so wrapped up in your models and misconceptions you couldn't recognize a miracle if it splattered you in your face. Here, look at this," she added, shoving her ring in front of my eyes. "What do you see?" She commanded an answer.

I looked at Hilda's ring and found myself drawn closer and closer to it as if by a magnet. It was a gold ring with a polished black stone set squarely on its upper surface. Inside the stone there appeared to be the face of a man. It was a negroid face, with thick lips and a thick, flat nose. He was wearing glasses and had short kinky hair. At first he was still, but slowly the man began to move and then he smiled. As a magician I was familiar with trickery, holograms and other devices of illusion, but the image in the ring defied all the principles I knew.

"Can I examine it?" I asked sheepishly.

Hilda removed the ring and tossed it to me for inspection. Now it seemed to be an ordinary ring. The image was gone.

"What is it? Where is it from?" I inquired with shock and curiosity.

"A *real* magician made that ring," Hilda chuckled. "His name is Sai Baba. *That's* who you should have seen when you were in India. Oh well, everything in its proper time," she said simply as she put the ring back on her finger.

She began caressing my head and I was immediately reminded of the special love that my grandmother and I shared for each other. "Hilda, I have so many unanswered questions. . ." I began to cry.

"Asking the questions is in itself the resistance to the answers," Hilda replied. "You must learn to meditate. The answers will come. Go home now. Come back when you can walk without the cane."

I said goodbye and, with tiny, shuffling steps, leaning on my cane, I walked out the door my brother held open for me.

In the car on the way back to New Jersey, Barry amplified one of the things Hilda had mentioned to me just before we left. "Hilda's path is meditation," he said. "It can't be taught, it has to be caught."

"What does that mean?" I asked.

"It's like this: you can't *try* to relax," he explained patiently, "but even though you can't *try* to relax, you *can* put yourself into an environment conducive to relaxation. If you hang around people who are uptight, it's bound to make you uptight. Spend time with calm people, and soon you'll begin to be calmer, too."

I didn't see what any of this had to do with meditation, and just as I was about to say so he looked over at me and smiled. "Breathe!" he commanded, with a touch of Hilda's authority.

It was only then I noticed that, in fact, I had hardly been breathing. How many years had I spent like this without realizing it — so tightly controlled and rigid that I would deprive myself of breath? Is that why Barry was talking to me about uptight people? Is that why Hilda was recommending that I "catch" meditation?

I had been given my life back, and I knew Hilda had been

right when she said it was a miracle. Slowly I was beginning to see that the reason I had been given back my life was in order to change it. The question was, how?

10

July found my legs almost completely healed. They were weak and severely scarred, portions still numb, but nonetheless, they worked. I had spent the previous month trying to meditate but the more I tried, the more hopeless it seemed. My mind chattered with thoughts and refused to be still. I felt I was a disappointment to my brother and Hilda.

The more I whipped myself into establishing a regimen for meditation, the more guilt I felt over failing. I believed that Barry and his friends who also studied with Hilda were more the "spiritual type" than I was, and I never really felt comfortable with them. At Hilda's weekly classes, which often numbered several hundred, I felt like a minority of one. The other students seemed to exemplify the epitome of spirituality: meditating, abstaining from meat, praying — all so effortlessly. The more I struggled, the more I heard phrases like "Don't push the river"; "Effort impairs the process"; and "Let go and let God." These words had no real meaning to me. I was trying so hard and judging my lack of progress so harshly that I wasn't ready to "let go" of anything.

One day a high school acquaintance of mine, Tom, stopped by to visit me on his way to the airport. In a few hours he was taking off for San Francisco. Since we had last seen each other, he had grown his hair, hippie-fashion, well past his shoulders and his beard reached halfway down his chest. When he entered my parents' living room, I was reading contracts, wondering whether or not to pick up where I had left off a few months earlier as Tolly the Clown. I had enough contracts to keep me traveling abroad for at least a year if that was the road I wanted to take.

"Shove the contracts," Tom counseled. "Come with me to San Francisco. That's where it's happening, man," he continued in hippie jargon. "You ought to split this scene." He placed a joint on the table. "Think it over," he added, winking as he left.

During my ten-year career, I had played 52 countries on five continents as Tolly the Clown Magician, and as I mulled over Tom's advice, I felt that he was right: that part of my life was finished. I picked up the joint from the table, lit it and inhaled. It wasn't the first time I had tried marijuana, but it had never affected me so strongly before. A tingle of well-being surged through my body and I began experiencing what I thought must be the sought-after state of consciousness for which Hilda prescribed meditation. "Hmmmmm," I pondered, "if I find getting here through meditation so difficult, why not employ alternatives?" I imagined seeing Tom wink at me once again, and I laughed.

Always an impulsive character, I flew to San Francisco 48 hours later. Tom met me at the airport and drove me to an apartment two blocks from the intersection of Haight and Ashbury. The apartment was furnished in modern "funk," with large cable spools for tables and magazine cutouts for wall decorations. Ten occupants shared the five rooms, and, as Tom's guest on an air mattress on the dining room floor, I was thrilled about making the transition into hippie heaven so easily.

Though Tom was accommodating, he had his own life in full

gear and I saw quite little of him. My other roommates were a mixture of students, dropouts, and welfare recipients. Only one held down a full-time job. Trying to make up for lost time — at age 24 I could've been a hippie for at least five years, I figured, if I'd been more on top of things — I bought a new pair of blue jeans, bleached them heavily, and then sandpapered the knees.

Like the others in my new home, I smoked pot daily, sometimes hourly. I also stopped shaving and never trimmed my hair. Within a few weeks I looked as if I truly belonged, but I seldom felt anything but lonely. Everyone in the apartment was cordial, but no one seemed to be reaching out to me with genuine gestures of friendship, so I spent most of my days exploring San Francisco, frequently wandering through the labyrinths of foliage in Golden Gate Park. The more I strained to make friends with my roommates, the more I seemed to be avoided. Jon, the youngest member of my new communal

SAN FRANCISCO, 1973

family, asked me quite frankly one day, "Why are you so up-tight man?" I was shocked: I wasn't aware that it showed. I thought my new facade had disguised my inner stress, but ob-viously I was wrong.

I rolled a joint and, smoking it with Jon, shared the story of my fragmented, depressing life. Most other people to whom I told the story thought I was making it up — especially the part about the library fund — but Jon listened attentively, emanating an aura of genuine compassion. Finally, he spoke. "Have you ever tripped?"

"Tripped?"

"Acid, mushrooms, peyote? You know, psychedelics?" he asked nonchalantly.

"No, never," I answered, quivering with fear, excitement and curiosity.

Jon went to the freezer and withdrew a packet of aluminum foil. From it he produced a miniscule square of what appeared to be clear plastic. "This is window pane, LSD-25, pure stuff," he said. "I don't know, maybe it'll help you. Since you've never tripped before, just take about a third. This is a pretty heavy dose." He shrugged and handed it to me almost reluctantly, again adding the warning, "Don't take it all. A third, maybe a half."

I scrutinized the innocent-looking chemical square in my palm. It measured about an eighth of an inch or so on each side. It seemed like a joke to divide it, but I took a razor blade and sliced it into two equal halves, placed one half on my tongue and put the other on a shelf in the kitchen. Thinking it best to have my cosmic experience in the arms of Mother Nature, I left the apart-ment and headed for Golden Gate Park. I walked through the fern groves and among the rainbows of flowers. An hour passed quickly, and though the walk was glorious, no unfamiliar sen-sations crept into my experience.

"How silly," I thought. "Obviously someone of my height and weight must need more than the microscopic dose I had consumed. Six feet and 165 pounds must certainly require the whole square!"

I returned to the apartment and ingested what remained of the mysterious "window pane." By now I was a bit skeptical, but I was still anticipating something. I sat on the living room couch and began flipping through the pages of some magazine when suddenly I noticed that my right foot was shaking violently. Jon had just entered the room and I could see that he was saying something to me, perhaps about my foot, but his words were unintelligible. Fear stabbed through my brain and the upper part of my body. I wanted to scream, cry, plead for help, but my vocal cords were frozen.

Inwardly, I was certain I had taken an overdose and would die. Tom's familiar face appeared and I was aware of Jon explaining to him what had happened. I sensed Tom being angry with Jon, and also sensed that they both felt helpless. All at once my jaw began to work: "I can't breathe!" I screamed. "I can't breathe! Help me! Help me!"

Tom sat down next to me and tried to explain that nothing could be done, I just had to wait for the chemical to work itself out of my system. He told me not to forget that the LSD trip was all a hallucination, and that when it was over I would be all right. Assuring me that my breathing was fine, he gave me some orange juice to sip, then reiterated: "Remember at all times that you're just hallucinating."

"How long will this last?" I asked pleadingly.

"Maybe six or seven hours," came his reply.

"No! Nooooo!" I screamed. Every muscle in my body seemed to be jumping in spasm. "I want it to stop! Please stop it!"

Tom brought me into a bedroom and told me to lie on the water bed. He put on soft music, lit a joint and helped guide it to my mouth. In between puffs, he administered some vitamin C and kept reassuring me that everything would be okay, all my distress would pass.

I closed my eyes and tried to relax by taking long, slow, deep breaths. I wasn't sure how much time had passed when I opened my eyes again. I looked around but could see absolutely nothing. No one was there but me, and the room was pitch black. The soft music was gone now, the stillness was complete; not even sounds of the traffic or other outside noises interrupted the quiet. "Am I dead?" I wondered.

Apprehension began rising in my body when suddenly blinding white light seered the retina of my eyes. The light was so intense I couldn't see. I blinked and tried to focus. When images finally began to appear, I realized that time was playing tricks with me: I was no longer in San Francisco, I was in Denville, New Jersey; it was just after I had tried to commit suicide for the first time and I was lying comatose in the hospital, Grandma and Valerie's mother just down the hall. My father was at my bedside and my heart had just ceased to beat. "His heart has stopped!" I heard my father shout.

The memory was so vivid that it wasn't a memory; I was living it again, completely. My senses were so taken over by the experience that it seemed as if I were in the coma again at the exact moment my heart stopped. But now, though apparently in the coma, I also became totally aware of everything that had transpired two-and-a-half years earlier during the time I had been in St. Clare's Hospital "unconscious."

As I lay there, I became conscious of a long tunnel extending from my navel, becoming narrower and narrower as it extended away from me. At the end of the tunnel was an opening so tiny that only my awareness could fit through it; everything else had to remain behind.

Gingerly, I allowed my awareness to separate from my body and to move toward this microscopic aperture. In the instant my consciousness sought to peer across the threshold, I was overwhelmed by the experience of BEING an asparagus. I *was* an asparagus: there was no conscious "me" separate from the experience; there were no thoughts, not even a reflection on how surprising, puzzling, or ridiculous this was, because there really wasn't anyone there to think about what was happening. I didn't even realize that "I" was having an experience. I had become asparagus-ness, absolute Asparagus Nature. The qualities of calmness, peacefulness and well-being come close to suggesting the condition in which I found myself, but I was well beyond even these states of tranquility. It was as if Bruce Tolly Burkan had never even existed, as if I had returned to a prior state, had never been human and had no frame of reference for humanness.

Up until then, it had never occurred to me that an asparagus, even without a mind or nervous system, could have awareness. Now I knew the truth by BEING it. While I was in the asparagus state, however, I wasn't labeling it "BEING an asparagus;" my intellect simply wasn't working. Only *after* the LSD trip in which I recalled the initial experience of asparagus-ness that had occurred while I was in the coma, could I think back with my intellect and reflect, "So that's what *BEING* an asparagus is all about."

Another aspect of this experience was equally important to expanding my understanding of the many levels of awareness that are part of all of us. When my consciousness first emerged from the tiny hole in the tunnel, I had a sudden awareness of being aware, and then, just as suddenly, an awareness of being aware of being aware. If it was "I" who was watching what was happening, then another watcher was watching the watcher. I *knew* then, on a deep level, that an impersonal witness, apart from anything I had ever experienced, was somehow contained within this mysterious place of *BEING* that previously I had only known to exist through my metaphysical reading. As this sense of knowing permeated me, softly in the distance I heard the echo of Ram Dass's voice: "Behind all *THAT*, here *we* are!"

This awareness lasted a moment. Then, for the next seven hours, while my body lay floating on the water bed, I was totally immersed in the asparagus place I now remember first visiting while in deep comas following each of my suicide attempts, and then again in the mental hospital when I was treated with electric shock and insulin coma therapy.

When I again became conscious of the water bed — and of having a body to which I was connected — Tom and Jon were in the room. They looked relieved as I greeted their anxious eyes with a grin. Neither of them spoke, but their silent nods seemed to acknowledge that I was now a member of some esoteric club. Still overwhelmed by the chemical magic, I couldn't really talk to them; the grin was about all I could muster in the way of communication. They left me alone to ponder the journey I had just taken and to integrate the experience of this altered state of consciousness into my previous thoughts and beliefs about life.

My first thoughts had to do with the books I'd read on Eastern mysticism. One word that appeared frequently in my reading was *maya*. I had always interpreted *maya* simply as a synonym for "illusion" or "illusory." I thought again about the analogy of the dream. Characters in a dream have no real substance, they are filmy projections from the dreamer's mind onto an imaginary screen upon which the action of the dream is observed. Oriental philosophers cite the witness or the watcher of the dream as being "real" and all else as being *maya*. The parallel is drawn that our everyday lives are merely projections from the One Mind of the Universe and what we erroneously label as "reality" is just *maya*. Now this had new meaning for me. Einstein's theory of relativity had already convinced me that energy and matter are really two forms of the same thing, and that the reason physicists haven't yet seen a subatomic particle is that these particles don't exist as "solid" entities but rather as energy patterns whose movements can only be observed in a cloud chamber. The ability to see through to this sub-sub-sub-sub atomic core of the metaphysical Universe, I now realized, reveals *maya*.

Until I had taken LSD, any such concepts had remained entirely in my intellect; now, for the first time, I had an experience of BEING the witness, of watching everything come and go while my awareness stood still, simply watching the *maya*-foam sudsing up and dissolving like bubbles of the ocean — being born, dying, changing constantly, always remaining the same; one moment everything seeming solid, the next, all becoming the filmy ether of a dream.

From the depths of the initial terror spawned in me by the acid, I now felt I had gained something very important. Not only did I now see the mystical concept of *maya* with new clarity, I felt a profound realization within the very cells of my body that *maya* is the substance of every physical manifestation behind which is the Oneness of the Universe. The LSD also put me in contact with the immortal *BEING* part of myself that is always there "Behind all *THAT!*" to use Ram Dass's words — *"THAT"* being the *maya* of my own body and the material world in which I live.

The LSD had made me "let go" totally — I had no choice but to surrender in its chemical wake — and as I passed into the state of asparagus-ness, I had an experience of what it was like not to *do* anything, simply to BE, and to let myself be aware of the many levels of awareness within me. This was a turning point in my life. Now my experience of who I was and what life was about was expansive and open-ended. Suddenly I *knew* there was a lot going on to which previously I had been totally blind.

11

Within the same month as my initiation to LSD, my brother, Barry, ever concerned with my well-being, came to San Francisco. Excitedly, I shared my psychedelic adventures with him. He, too, was a member of the "club" and neither criticized nor congratulated me for taking the plunge. While sightseeing together one day, we stopped in front of a colorful poster stapled to a telephone pole. "MEETING OF THE WAYS!" it announced, and went on to describe a consciousness-raising symposium consisting of a host of speakers, workshops, activities and displays. The event was several days away. Barry suggested we attend and I agreed. While continuing our walk through the city, we found a metaphysical bookshop with an extensive collection of used books. Barry bought a paperback for fifteen cents, and we returned home.

The book, *Handbook to Higher Consciousness*, fascinated me. The author was Ken Keyes, and he offered a smorgasbord of recipes for happiness: a smattering of Buddhism, Hinduism and other Eastern philosophies as well as a variety of other concepts, many of which I'd seen before. The novelty was to read the practical ways in which he integrated these ideas into everyday situations.

A major part of Ken Keyes's work seemed to focus on how to avoid accumulating stress as we go about our daily lives. This was particularly apt for me for whom, in the past, every mistake was judged to be a major mistake and every problem a life-wrenching trauma. The book struck me as straightforward and refreshing, and I felt the author was a wise man with much to teach. When later that night I was looking over the poster for the "Meeting of the Ways" symposium, I was more than overjoyed to discover that Key Keyes was a scheduled speaker.

The day of the symposium arrived, coinciding with the Autumnal Equinox of 1973, and I remember feeling that the Equinox was marking a transition not only into the new season of fall, but into a new season in my life, too.

The "Meeting of the Ways" turned out to be a circus of consciousness-raising groups from all sectors of the western United States. Spiritual people of every description had stalls vending books, incense, statues and photographs of Saints, Masters and Holy Men. The carnival-like atmosphere made me smile more than once. "This really is my kind of church," I mused to myself.

Late in the afternoon, Ken Keyes gave a brief talk, the essence of which was, *"You create your own reality."* As he explained this simple statement, my heart began to palpitate. I realized that the "missing ingredient" for which I had been searching so long was materializing right now in front of me. Ken was literally handing me on a silver platter *the* thing I had never been able to find on my own and the absence of which had twice made me decide that life wasn't worth living. Quite simply, he was telling me that I could choose anything I wanted and it would come to me because, in fact, I created my own experience of myself. Regardless of the situations or circumstances in which I found myself, I and I alone created my responses and reactions, and this meant that I and I alone — whether I was conscious of it or not — created my own experience of these situations or circumstances.

I had always looked outside myself for both the answers to my problems and the responsibility for creating them. If I was miserable, it was external circumstances, I believed, that had made me that way; if I sought enlightenment, I also expected it to be "out there." That was why I had gone to India to seek the Masters — because I wanted *them* to enlighten me. It had never occurred to me that it was my own attitude that perpetuated my misery even when external circumstances might have brought rejoicing; similarly, it had never occurred to me that if I wanted enlightenment I would have to seek it solely within myself.

As I sat in the darkened auditorium, I began to see that I could have whatever I wanted in life, but first I had to be really clear about what it was I wanted. Once I created the intention, *anything* could be mine: I myself would become the magnet that would ultimately bring it all to me. If I wanted to be a spiritual person I had to begin with the realization that I already was one, and to let the process of unfolding my spiritual nature happen in its own time.

Ken reminded everyone that no matter what the situation was in our lives, *we* created it that way. Once we begin to see our own part in creating our lives, and we begin to stop blaming others — which also means that we stop seeing ourselves as victims — then and only then can we begin to zero in on *how* we are doing "it" to ourselves, and how to go about *changing* the things we find unacceptable.

Ken concluded by pointing out that we create as much suffering in the world when we take offense as when we give offense. His remarks made me realize how strange it was that up until that moment I had never stopped to see how much suffering I was causing for myself every time I took offense because of what someone else did or said. It seemed that every time I saw a chance to suffer, I went for it like fish for bait. Ken didn't seem to have this problem. Throughout his talk, he beamed like a man who was truly happy. The impact of his radiance was overwhelming, especially since he was completely paralyzed from the neck down and he spoke to us from a wheelchair. At fifty-three years of age, he had been in a wheelchair half his life, as a result of polio. He had to be washed, dressed, moved and fed by others. His presence alone made such an impression on me that I resolved to see him again as soon as possible.

12

The following week, Barry and I took a bus across the Bay Bridge to "The Living Love Center," a huge house that had formerly belonged to one of the fraternities of the University of California at Berkeley, and which now served as an office and teaching facility for Ken and a home for him and several of his students. During my visit I learned that the Center was in need of a gardener. I immediately begged for the position. Ten days later, Barry returned to New Jersey and I moved in with Ken to become his student and gardener.

Having spent his early adulthood in the Navy and then aboard a yacht, Ken ran the Center exactly like a ship. Everything was accomplished effortlessly as a result of following a routine each day. I found it a comfortable environment. We got up early, did morning exercises, cleaned the premises, then sat in class while Ken taught us different aspects of Eastern philosophy as he interpreted them. The daily instruction was useful and practical, never abstract. As days passed into weeks, I felt something tight within myself beginning to relax... at last! After two suicide

KEN KEYES

attempts, electric shock therapy, insulin coma treatments and pounds of drugs, with the help of this brilliant and loving man in a wheelchair I was finally lowering my guard and changing into the person I had always wanted to be.

A major part of this was learning how to use my mind so that I could get up each day and choose what I wanted to experience. I could resolve that no matter what circumstances arose, I would be able to meet them in a positive way. I began to see I could either enjoy everything that happened in the course of that day or I could use it to teach me a lesson. These were not mere words: the more I put them into practice, the more I began to see how true they were. It *was* up to me how I reacted to the events in my life and whether I wanted to *learn* from "mistakes" and things that "went wrong" or would prefer just to suffer and blame.

I also began to use the process of visualization to help me reach my goals. This involved focusing the power of my mind by closing my eyes and breathing deeply for a few minutes to attain a relaxed state and then, with my imagination, "seeing" what I wanted to happen as if it were already occurring. The process reminded me of the Bible passage, "As above, so below;" if I could see it with my mind's eye above, I could manifest it in the physical world below.

It was wonderful to picture the things I *wanted* to happen. Like so many people, I used to picture things I dreaded without ever once realizing that by visualizing these things I had taken the first step toward making them happen. Where before I had fixed my imagination on negativity, Ken demanded that I, along with the other students, focus my thoughts on love, service, health, harmony and happiness. The more I followed these instructions, the more deeply I realized the truth of the first lecture I had heard him give — that how I viewed myself and the world around me had everything to do with what my day-to-day life would be like.

After class, I would go outside to perform my chores as resident gardener. I had told Ken initially that I knew almost nothing about gardening, but I had promised to do research, ask questions if I was unsure of something, and work hard. The grounds had not been cared for in years. I removed garbage from the stream that flowed through the property, picked up broken glass that had been pounded into the dirt, trimmed and uprooted sticker bushes and cleared areas for planting. Though the routine was lacklustre and strenuous, I was ecstatic. I felt as if I had finally attained a lifelong dream. After all, it is a greater blessing to be the garbage man in Heaven than the richest man in Hell.

Once a month, Ken invited the public at large to spend a weekend in his home and to participate in a seminar he had devised to illustrate the teachings in his books. During the first of these seminars I attended, Ken told everybody present — about twenty of us — to remove our clothes and sit in a large circle. One at a time, we were instructed to stand in the middle and tell the group the one thing we liked most about our bodily appearance and the one thing we liked least.

I was shocked by his request. I tried to act nonchalant; inside, I was quaking. I had never done such an outrageous thing before, and I found myself wondering if this might even be illegal and would lead to all of us being thrown in jail. I wondered if I was alone in my shock or if other people were equally apprehensive about this *avant-garde* exercise. After all, I was a New Jersey boy; nothing this racy had ever crept into my realm of experience. Perhaps Californians were more used to disrobing in front of a whole room full of people? I kept my eyes focused downwards, but soon sensed that others, too, were as nervous as I was; the odor all around me indicated perspiration was being released in large amounts.

One by one the participants entered the center of the ring and announced that they didn't like the shape of their paunches or the size of their penis, rejected their baldness, bulges, big hips, small or large breasts or crooked nose. Some liked their smile, loved their beard, ears or eyes. It was ironic to watch two women talk about themselves right after each other, and hear that the first didn't like her breasts because she thought they were too big while the second, who was of the exact same build, lamented that hers were too small.

Ken was naked, too, and after seeing how accepting he was of his withered limbs it became harder for me and the others not to accept our own bodies. After each presentation, he made a humorous comment, and what I had thought would be a "heavy" experience turned out to be light and comical. The conclusion of the exercise clearly demonstrated what Hilda had implied and Ram Dass had told me, that behind all our bodies, "here *we* are."

Gradually, as we experienced ourselves with the perspective gained by looking through Ken's eyes, we began to discover who we really were apart from who we were programmed to believe we were. The entire process of "show and tell" took about an hour. It was a simple but profound lesson and by the time it was over, everyone, including myself, felt quite comfortable with our naked bodies exposed for all to see. We laughed uproariously at the insight that actually we are always naked, under our clothes, that is. Our feelings and souls are always laid bare for sensitive eyes to see, no matter how we try to hide them. Despite my sleeping on a mattress in the hippie apartment, bleaching my blue jeans and letting my hair grow, hadn't Jon spotted how uptight I had really been?

Within weeks of moving to The Living Love Center, I felt like a different person. I was open to learning new ideas, hearing new viewpoints, and seemed to be enjoying life more than at any time I could remember. Old concepts took on new meaning under Ken's tutelage. Little by little we bridged the roles of teacher and student and started to become friends. Before his study of Buddhism led him to realize he wanted to be a teacher, Ken had been a successful real estate broker. Since my parents were also real estate brokers, we often found ourselves having conversations, generally satirical, on the subject of real estate. At times like these, he and I locked into each other's mind in a way that made us appreciate each other in a very personal way. As the months progressed, Ken reduced my responsibilities in the garden and invited me to work with him on planning the format for his upcoming workshops.

Drawing on my experience in show business, I shared with Ken my impression that his seminar was somewhat dull and offered to help him add some pizzaz. He was delighted to have threatrical input, and soon the seminar became a real show. There were brightly colored placards and displays and comedy skits to highlight concepts Ken taught. I started by doing the "warm up," rang the dinner bell, handled special problems, administered the schedule and took care of logistics. Within a few months, I was doing everything but the main teaching work. With this new show business energy, Ken himself became a more powerful and entertaining speaker.

The joy in our relationship and the dynamics of the retailored format affected everyone attending the seminars, and soon word-of-mouth created a waiting list to get in. Eventually, Ken gave me large chunks of time to speak, since my past life of misery, contrasted with my present happiness, was a moving demonstration of the possibility of change, and people found it inspiring. It felt good to share these experiences, knowing that I was giving other people courage to create a more positive future for themselves.

Soon we took the seminar on the road throughout California, and it met with rave reviews. Next we co-authored a book, an ABCs of consciousness growth, *How to Make Your Life Work or Why Aren't You Happy?*, which became a best-seller. I then pressed Ken to form a nationwide network for his teaching to include newsletters, lectures and seminars all over the country. As our work continued to expand, I danced about with a sense of freedom I had only dreamt of before. I was in love with Ken, in love with life and, for the first time, almost in love with myself. Looking back now I can see that this was the point in my life after which thoughts about suicide never again crept into my mind — and it should be noted that changing from someone who was hellbent on killing himself into a person who *never again* entertained such thoughts was a monumental transformation. Ken had, indeed, given me the missing ingredient: he showed me how to create my life as a positive experience.

My enthusiastic planning had its effect, and soon The Living Love Center was drawing workshop participants from as far away as New York, Florida and Europe. An exciting year unfolded for me as Ken's right-hand man. Finally I was enjoying what seemed to be permanent happiness.

My evolution was enhanced by my associating so closely and so continuously with other people committed to spiritual growth. Living communally at The Living Love Center made it easier to integrate insights I was having about my own behavior patterns. The fact that Ken provided the environment, the structure and the tools for me to make real progress in transforming myself made me deeply grateful to him. The tools he provided were particularly effective for me because he spoke directly to my intellect, and I was used to dealing with the world intellectually, rather than on a feeling level. Although I knew instinctively where it was that Hilda and Ram Dass were trying to guide me, it wasn't until I began to study with Ken that I felt empowered to get there on my own. Hilda and Ram Dass offered me a path of heart, but my heart was too closed then to make any real progress; Ken's path of the mind eventually enabled me to open my heart so that I could receive what Hilda and Ram Dass had to offer.

I was also deeply grateful that in Ken I finally found someone whom I genuinely wanted to be like, someone whose career, lifestyle and service to others provided me with a model to emulate. The more I changed, the more I began to feel that I wanted to share what I was learning with others as a teacher, even though I knew I was still only a student.

13

Although I was now clear that I wanted to make teaching my career, first I had to overcome my own initial skepticism. After all, only a year before I had been chronically suicidal. "How could anybody so screwed up hope to teach anyone anything?" I wondered. Fortunately, Ken was an expert in creating teachers, even from former psychological basket cases. He taught me, and anyone else who was eager to learn, how to use an ancient tool to measure, support and provide a road map for spiritual growth.

Ken explained this concept in terms of what he called "the seven centers of consciousness." I had already heard these seven centers referred to as *chakras* by Hilda, Ram Dass, and my brother, Barry. Each *chakra,* I had been told, was related to a different ray of spiritual energy. All of this seemed very mystifying to me. The way Ken described the seven centers of consciousness made it easy for me to understand what they might have to do with myself and my life. It was a tremendous personal breakthrough to realize that spiritual growth, which before had so overwhelmed me with its apparent complexity, could be described according to a seven-point system that would let me see exactly *where I was spiritually at any moment.*

Since then, I have come to see these seven points as actual *Life Requirements* for anyone who wants to develop his or her fullest potential as a human being. Listed in ascending order, these seven Requirements are: 1) *Financial Security;* 2) *Good Feelings;* 3) *Self-worth;* 4) *Active Compassion;* 5) *Creative Expression;* 6) *Attentive Awareness;* and, 7) *Constant Connectedness.*

In my own teaching today, I report what I've learned from my experience: we don't need all seven requirements to be happy, but there's much more to life than mere happiness. Although until age twenty-five I believed happiness was almost too much to hope for, through my work with Ken I began to realize that happiness is not so difficult to attain once a person understands a few basic rules. Beyond happiness, however, is the spiritual dimension. The more of the seven Life Requirements we make our own, the more spiritually enlightened we become. The more spiritually enlightened we become, the closer we are to true joy.

In more detail, these steps on the spiritual ladder look like this:

1. *Financial Security.* For those of us who are not saints, it's impossible to remain in a happy state of mind if there is no money for basic necessities such as food, clothes and shelter. How can any person who is constantly worrying about his next meal be happy? Before anything else, we must provide means to sustain ourselves.

2. *Good Feelings.* Once we are no longer preoccupied with security on a material level, we next require a certain amount of pleasant sensations in our daily lives. Satisfying friendships, food, music, sex, long walks or anything that makes us feel good physically or emotionally can provide the sensations we need for life to feel worthwhile.

3. *Self-worth.* After satisfying our basic needs for security and good feelings, we then need to feel a sense of self-esteem, free

from guilt and unworthiness. *Self-worth* isn't to be confused with egotism or exaggerated pride; instead, it is a deep sense of our own value, uniqueness and ability to perform effectively. People who don't have a positive self-image feel powerless to control their own destinies. They can have all the money and wonderful sensations imaginable and yet they will never be happy. When we don't have *Self-worth*, we are constantly threatened by people and situations around us, and always seem to be defending ourselves and our territory. Whether we show it or not, we get angry easily; we build ourselves up by putting others down either verbally or mentally — and still we continue feeling bad about ourselves.

4. *Active Compassion.* This quality stems from love — not the stereotyped love portrayed in romantic novels, but the love that flows out of us and results in good deeds directed toward other people.

The love that makes our hearts go pitter-pat and causes our loins to twitch isn't love, but a sensation, and belongs in the second category of Life Requirements, *Good Feelings.* The love that is the source of *Active Compassion* allows us to forgive the past both for ourselves and others. It enables us to forget the pettiness and traumas of yesterday. Our love for our mates, our children, our friends, is really only the beginning; the love that forms the basis of *Active Compassion* is an embodiment of succeeding with the first three Life Requirements and loving ourselves enough to let energy flow through our hearts. As this state unfolds within us and becomes full, humility and compassion are natural results.

Active Compassion is synonymous with charity. It is a way of receiving through giving. It is serving others because we have feelings of good will toward our fellow human beings and know that they are serving us by allowing us to serve them. I once saw a poster that stated simply: "Love is an active verb." Until we start performing good deeds for their own sake, not for praise or for other personal reward, or because we think we should, we can't progress up the path toward enlightenment. It is possible to garner moments of pleasure from life if we satisfy the first three Life Requirements alone, but joy with a capital "J" comes only after we consider someone else's needs to be as important as our own. It is in this area that Ken provided me with my greatest opportunities: I served him completely and in so doing I experienced this Joy from service. Physically arduous and exacting tasks performed on his behalf made me tingle with gratitude.

Even though I had spent years serving others by volunteering in hospitals as a clown magician, I learned from Ken that it was important first to love myself, so that I was no longer serving others in order to compensate for what I considered to be my general inadequacy. The discovery of *Active Compassion,* love flowing forth in service, was a great lesson for me.

5. *Creative Expression.* Whether this creativity comes in the form of music, dance, art, song, writing or some other hobby or vocation, including business, we must somehow unlock our creative capacity. Otherwise, even if the other four Life Requirements have been met sufficiently, we will lapse into boredom. Our need for *Creative Expression* is so subtle that when it is missing, many people can't even figure out where the problem lies. And yet, when creativity manifests itself in full bloom, it perfumes one's life as if by magic.

It is possible for Life Requirements to overlap or coincide: the way in which we channel our creativity can also be the way in which we serve others or earn our living. When this occurs, life is experienced as a cornucopia from which we always have more than we need. The inner sensation of this is one of abundance and fulfillment; our *life* becomes our *Creative Expression.*

6. *Attentive Awareness.* Just before this point is reached, we may feel happy enough that we lack any great incentive to explore the remaining two areas of growth. But *Attentive Awareness* provides a profound dimension to happiness that

connects us directly to our inner spiritual nature. If we only satisfy our yearnings for the first five Life Requirements, although we may feel nourished, we may still remain uneasy when the subjects of birth, death, God, or inexplicable phenomena are discussed in our presence.

Attentive Awareness means PAYING ATTENTION *moment by moment.*

Using *Attentive Awareness,* each person can look within and discover his or her own inner Truth. As we pay attention to who we are within — the "Behind all *THAT,* here *we* are" that Ram Dass first told me about — spirituality evolves. *Attentive Awareness* kindles a spiritual awakening that results in "ordinary" moments no longer seeming ordinary.

Paying attention enables us to cope with life's seemingly contradictory and paradoxical nature. It enables us to be aware of our egos and see them clearly. It permits us to step back from the melodrama of our lives and watch it all unfold as if on a movie screen. It creates the needed detachment to laugh at our own foibles and shortcomings.

Quite simply, *Attentive Awareness,* the sixth Life Requirement, guides us into being aware that we are aware. This creates a bridge into the spiritual dimension, and allows us to see our true nature as being separate from the cycle of birth, life-scramble and death. The fulfillment that accompanies *Attentive Awareness* is so far above the satisfaction provided by the first five Life Requirements that it resembles it no more than a butterfly resembles a caterpillar.

This was the realm for which Hilda recommended meditation, and which I initially discovered with drugs. Once found, it can be returned to by any number of effective means, including bio-feedback devices, sensitivity training and spontaneous insights. My primary means today is meditation.

7. *Constant Connectedness.* This seventh Life Requirement is the most elusive, and, therefore, the most difficult to describe. So few people incorporate it into their lives that it is rare to find

an effective model. In fact, it was only after my second visit to India, four years after I left Ken and The Living Love Center, that I encountered Swami Sathya Sai Baba, whose existence revealed to me for the first time what the seventh Life Requirement was about. When attained, this mode of living — constantly feeling connected to every person and thing on the planet, experiencing a connection to the Power of the entire Universe — enables a person to perceive not merely the world of solid objects but the *maya* itself, the bundles of energy and particles appearing as form. Nothing lies beyond our comprehension if we discover and develop this aspect of our nature. As students of life, it stands before us as a monument to our potential as human beings, and explains to us all the powers attributed to the saints and sages throughout history.

The way I learned to use this seven-point system at The Living Love Center was very simple. Ken would remind us throughout the day to pay attention to what was going on in our minds. He taught us that the ego is that part of the mind that keeps us stuck in trying to satisfy the first three Life Requirements: *Financial Security, Good Feelings,* and *Self-Worth.* By observing which area dominates our consciousness most, we can know where we stand on the spiritual path. If my mind was worrying about money and bills, obviously I was trying to satisfy the first Life Requirement, *Financial Security.* If I was thinking about how many hours a week I could use for community service, then I was involving myself in the fourth Life Requirement, *Active Compassion.* Whenever I felt unfulfilled, I just had to see which of the seven Life Requirements I was overlooking.

Using this method didn't only help me to see where I was on the path now that I was with Ken, it also helped me to understand where my consciousness had been in the past when I was so severely depressed. When I had felt worst about myself, I had *always* been thinking about money, things, sensations, and my self-image.

Without *Self-Worth,* I couldn't really enjoy material security or even the physical sensations of sex, except fleetingly; I couldn't have a deep appreciation for beauty no matter how many sights I saw on my excursions around the world. Of course, I hadn't learned to use *Attentive Awareness* to find out what I was doing to perpetuate this state. My constant judgments and prescriptions for how I should be acting got in the way of paying sufficient attention to my behavior to learn anything from it.

After almost a year in Ken's commune, I was a different person. I finally felt equipped to handle any situation life could deal me, because more and more frequently I was using every life situation as an opportunity for growth.

As for my desire to become a teacher, Ken had promoted me to a position in which I often conducted seminars myself, with him appearing only occasionally to give a brief talk. My dream was coming true, and I was proud; too proud.

Naturally, I was the last to notice the problem. I was so elated with my own good feelings and growing self-respect I never noticed that my ego had now begun to delude me with self-importance. I was the one who played the role of seminar leader in a seminar designed to help people to reduce their ego. People respected my effectiveness in helping them to eliminate restricting ego patterns, but, like a medicine that can turn to poison in too large a dosage, I became an intimidating character who didn't turn off even when not involved in seminars. In my own eyes, I was a noble servant while in seminars, and, outside seminars, a frank friend.

Trapped in my own ego patterns, I soon began using other people for my personal pleasure. I misused my position of authority as a seminar leader and frequently seduced participants into my bedroom, asking one young woman after another at the close of the seminars up to my room "to see the sunset." I experimented with every drug I could find and never had second thoughts. Often, I did the right things for the wrong reasons. I decided to fast, for example, not because I understood that it would clean out my body of toxins I had accumulated through bad eating habits and the multitude of drugs I had ingested over the years, but because I thought fasting was something spiritual people do. When I fasted, I took great pleasure in announcing to people I was "in my ninth day," knowing they would react with awe at my "spirituality." I even took pleasure in hearing a rumor — which I didn't bother to contradict — that I never slept.

I was on a power trip for months before it was brought to my attention. The euphoria of drugs and the pleasures of promiscuity prevented me from seeing clearly. Occasionally I glimpsed the truth, but I would immediately fall into not paying attention and thus never had a sustained realization of it. It has been written that "He who knows not, but knows not that he knows not, is a fool; he who knows not, but knows that he knows not, is a student; he who knows, but knows not that he knows, is asleep; he who knows and knows that he knows, is wise." By that definition, I was a fool.

It took the shock of sudden illness to bring me to a new awareness of where I had bogged down on the path. Only when I was too sick to get out of bed to play my ego-inflating games was I finally able to hear what people had been telling me for so long: I hadn't been doing the seminars for others as service, I had been doing them for my own self-aggrandizement. I suddenly saw how blind I had been — and yet, even seeing this, humility was still a lesson I didn't even realize had to be learned.

I contracted what I thought was the flu, but it refused to go away, even after weeks of ravaging my body. I lost more and more weight, and found myself sleeping most of the day. Before any of this had begun, however, at Ken's encouragement I registered for the EST training. He was very impressed with it and wanted me to share its benefits. And, of course, anything learned there would ultimately add to the quality of our workshops. As the date for the EST training approached, I was still disabled by illness. Nevertheless, not daring to "break an agreement," and certainly not with Werner Erhard and the EST

Organization, I attended the first weekend, which was just as wonderful as Ken had told me it would be. In the middle of the week, while waiting for test results on my mysterious and lingering illness, I discovered a sizable mass in my scrotum.

My doctor summoned me to his office. He was a likable fellow who probably envisioned himself being fatherly toward his patients. He rambled on about a tumor and the urgent need for surgery. Inside, I was thinking how much God must love me to put me constantly in positions that had so much potential for consciousness growth. Not only did I fail to react as the doctor expected, I even had a trace of a smile on my face as I thought about my remarkable melodrama.

There was some irony in my current situation, of course. Before, when I was miserable, I had tried to kill myself. Now, when I was happy, and I realized how very much I wanted to live, I was forced to face death. I sat back in the doctor's office that day, musing to myself, "Hmmmmm, I wonder how this is going to go."

Assuming that my composure indicated a lack of understanding, the doctor finally said with an expression of darkest gravity, "You have cancer! I want to operate immediately!"

When I got home I found myself calling the EST Organization to inform them that I wouldn't be completing the second weekend because I was about to undergo cancer surgery. A voice on the other end of the phone replied: "Are you willing to accept responsibility for creating this as a way to avoid completing the EST training?"

14

I flew back to New Jersey for my surgery. Barry immediately wanted me to see Hilda. "She's healed so many people of cancer," he said encouragingly. But the day after my return I was hospitalized. The phone rang in my room before I had even finished changing into the hospital gown for the X-rays. It was Hilda. "Don't worry about a thing," she said with levity. "Cancer is my specialty."

Truthfully, I was no more worried now than I was at the moment I had first heard the words, "You have cancer." Since that time I had done some intensive soul-searching and I had concluded that death really was not a formidable threat to me. If I died, I died. And if I survived, I felt a deep inner sense that I could bring some good into the world and some insight into the lives of people floundering in despair. I had witnessed the effect my lectures and seminars had on people, and it was good. The shortcoming in my work as a teacher was my ego. I felt that if I lived, that would no longer be a problem. The quiet days I had spent alone before going into the hospital had revealed so much. I was growing, evolving into someone I could finally hold in high regard.

Even though I could now see how conceited I had become, I didn't condemn myself; I simply realized it was something I had to overcome if I wanted to grow. Ken had given me a method to observe how I was creating my reality and how I could change it. As I looked at myself, I realized I was overindulging in the third Life Requirement. For so many years I had been starving for a sense of self-esteem that once I had begun to experience it, my hunger for it was ravenous. The point was to achieve a balance where along with Self-worth I would also have humility.

As I lay in my hospital bed, I often thought of Hilda, whose life was a symbol of *Active Compassion*. Not only did she refuse to accept money for her teaching — and her weekly class often numbered 800 — she was also available 24 hours a day to anyone in need. It gradually began to dawn on me what the purpose of my own life really was.

I figured that if twice I had elected to throw my life away, the one I now had really didn't belong to me. If I wanted to use it selfishly for my own personal gain or ego satisfaction, then certainly it *would* be taken away. Intuitively I knew that if in all sincerity I was willing to acknowledge that the life I now had belonged to humanity, that if I dedicated it to service and charity, it would not be taken from me. More than any time before, I had a sense of God *within* me, and despite what appeared to be a very critical situation, I relaxed, "let go and let God."

I didn't visualize God as a bearded entity with any resemblance to a human being. Rather, I felt much as a nursing infant might feel when chaos and noise are bombarding his room in the midst of a war: guns, bombs, screaming everywhere, but through it all, the infant sucking his mother's breast knows only warmth, security, peace and a feeling of being connected to the Source, safe and protected. For me, God was an unseen breast that constantly nourished me.

I had heard a story about a local Judge whose son had committed murder. Before the trial, the Judge's wife pleaded with him to remember that the boy on trial was their son. "But I'm the Judge," rumbled the husband. "But he's your son," reminded the wife. "But I'm the Judge," the reply came again. "But he's your son," the woman reiterated. I suppose that, for many, God is like the father in this tale, but for me, I began to sense God as the mother, infinitely compassionate, never judging. I felt God as a warm, friendly, loving feeling, caressing me, forgiving and never threatening me. During my illness, I was infused with trust for the Divine and felt no trepidation over what could have easily been labeled as my past "sins."

After a day of extensive tests and X-rays, I was exhausted. The doctor entered my room in early evening and informed me the operation would take place the following day. I perceived that my cheerfulness disarmed him. My cheerfulness was only a reflection of the happiness I had finally discovered within myself. Someone can easily be *content* when everything around him is comfortable; *happiness*, however, as I was now experiencing it, revealed itself as independent of outside circumstances. It really didn't matter to me what the outcome of the surgery was. I was able to watch it as if it were a soap opera; I was only casually interested in how the story would end. Getting more and more frustrated, my doctor explained that regardless of the extent to which the cancer had spread, he would have to remove my testicles. Hopefully, it had not yet spread to my lymph system. Nonetheless, my lower abdomen would be opened first so that the lymph channels could all be inspected and clamped prior to incising my scrotum. He placed a release form in front of me for my signature.

"Before I sign this, doctor, I have a question. When you remove my testicles, aren't you going to replace them with some sort of plastic substitute?" I asked.

"You're referring to a prosthesis," the doctor replied. "No, this is a small hospital and we don't have that particular prosthesis."

"What about your supplier?" I inquired. "Surely you must have access to them."

"Usually we do, but this is a weekend and the surgical supplier is closed," he said unconvincingly.

"Well, doctor," I began, "let me explain something that you may find a bit difficult to understand. You see, I live in a commune and we are frequently naked around each other. I like the aesthetics of my body appearing whole. What I'm trying to say is that I'm more attached to the prosthesis than I am to my life at this point, so we'll just have to wait until Monday for the surgery." I pushed the unsigned release form back onto his side of the table.

The doctor, visibly shaken by my lightheartedness, tried to persuade me. "Mr. Burkan, waiting two days could mean the difference between the cancer remaining localized or entering your lymph system. I don't think you understand —"

"Doctor," I interrupted, "I don't think *you* understand. Until I see the prosthesis with my own eyes, I'm not signing the release." He left the room, stymied.

Within an hour my phone rang. It was my mother. She had been called by my doctor and had been enlisted to aid him in his attempt to get my signature on the all-important paper that would release him from any responsibility if the operation failed. My mother pleaded, but I was adamant.

Early the next morning a young orderly entered my room with a razor. "I'm here to prepare you for surgery," he said introducing himself.

Jokingly, I pointed to the razor. "Are *you* going to cut off my balls?"

The quip made him laugh. "No, I'm here to shave you and apply iodine to your skin."

"I think there's some misunderstanding," I began, "I haven't signed a medical release."

"I heard about it," the orderly smiled. "We've *all* heard about it. Your doctor made some phone calls and found a hospital about seventy miles from here with the prosthesis. It'll arrive by ambulance any minute."

The phone jangled and Hilda's sweet voice was soon in my ear. "Tolly dear, we've all been praying for you. Now you must use the power of your own mind. Every particle and atom of this Universe is connected. The greatest force which exists is available to you right now through thought. Use your mind to rearrange the atoms in your body."

"Rearrange my atoms? How do I do that?" I asked.

"Just *pretend* that you are rearranging your atoms with your imagination. Use your mind to visualize yourself healthy and whole. Start imagining that all cancerous growth is diminishing, diminishing, diminishing, becoming a mere nothing; leaving your body forever. Your atoms *will* rearrange themselves. Vibrate the inner tissues of your body by chanting the word 'Om-m-m.' Let the sound resonate inside you. Turn that tumor into water and eliminate it through your kidneys. Rearrange your atoms!" she repeated.

The orderly finished his work and I filled my entire abdominal cavity with breath. "Om-m-m-m-m-m-m-m," I intoned, allowing the buzz of the sound to resonate in my body. "Om-m-m-m-m-m-m-m." Even though there was doubt in my mind that such a simple process could have the profound results Hilda promised, I focused my imagination and actually began to visualize my atoms rearranging themselves.

My mother and father entered the room just as I stopped "Om-m-m-m-ming" and was opening my eyes. "Did you sign the paper?" my father implored.

"I won't sign it until I see the prosthesis," I said, not wanting to distress him, but not knowing how to avoid it.

A stretcher was wheeled beside my bed and I asked if it wasn't premature since no release forms had been signed. The nurse told me that both the prosthesis and the papers would arrive at the operating room about the same time as I would, and I was whisked away in a bustle of starched, white uniforms.

When I arrived at the operating room, my doctor and his surgical team were awaiting me in hospital green. A small box was placed under my nose and the doctor proudly announced, "The prosthesis!" I looked into the box and saw two rubbery eggs not much larger than oversized jelly beans. "Oh no, doctor," I chided, "these won't do. They're the wrong size."

The doctor became florid while his team struggled to surpress their smiles. "Mr. Burkan," he said, trying to maintain his composure, "there will be tissue build-up I assure you. No one will ever notice. *Pleeease* sign the paper." I did so and was promptly anesthetized back into asparagus. "Om-m-m-m-m-m" was on my lips as I faded away.

Several hours later I opened my eyes. An incision had been made in my abdomen and my scrotum. I will simply report the facts of what transpired that Saturday morning in 1974. When the surgeons peeked and poked inside, the tumor that had clearly been observed on X-rays and had orchestrated the entire melodrama was nowhere to be found. Furthermore, the incisions made on Saturday were completely healed by the following Tuesday, and on Friday I celebrated by going mountain climbing. The rubbery eggs never left their cardboard nest.

Within two weeks I was back in California. The doctor who had first diagnosed my condition and who was in charge of my postoperative care simply congratulated me on my spontaneous remission. I was surprised that he wasn't more surprised, but he explained that there were many, many documented cases very similar to mine. I wondered how many of these other people attributed their healing to connecting with the Source, through their own minds.

ONE WEEK AFTER SURGERY

15

I returned to The Living Love Center jubilant and determined not to repeat the mistakes of my past. My life, which I once had perceived as wretched, now inspired me and I felt an obligation to share my process of transformation so that other people might be encouraged. Somehow, I had a feeling that I had "arrived" someplace, that I was "finished." The folly of *that* thought would catch up to me later, but for the time being, I was blithe, grateful, and in awe.

I resumed my role as seminar leader in Ken's continually growing organization. The insights I had received were a challenge to communicate, so I devised games, talks, activities and other procedures to take people from one stage of consciousness into another, so that they would experience for themselves the same revelations I had experienced since meeting Hilda, Ram Dass and Ken. Seeing the constant growth in workshop attendance, it seemed that I was successful. I took my work to heart; it was the career I had felt could never really exist for me.

"Attachment is the root cause of all suffering," I would say, quoting Buddha with a new understanding.

It is our attachment to ideas, models and narrow expectations that causes us to demand that life conform to our
preconceived notions. We are addicted to controlling what
happens, and when something happens in a way that is different from the way we desire it to happen, we reject it. If only
we could reject nothing, welcome every experience either by
enjoying it or learning from it, suffering would evaporate from
our lives. Every life situation is an opportunity for growth —
even pain, I had discovered.

I talked about the physical pain I had experienced after my
surgery, and how I had decided to use *Attentive Awareness* on
it rather than to reject it by requesting pain killers. Pain, of course,
is the one thing no one accepts easily. I dealt with it by telling
myself that what I was feeling was only a sensation. First, I
visualized the pain as having colors, and then I imagined it to
be tiny forms like elves and little dragons, running around my
body. Soon, the pain was dancing about me as if it were a media
show. Then I merged with the pain by using my total awareness.
Now I used the pain as a point on which to focus. Instead of
rejecting it, I was simply paying attention to it, accepting it, experiencing it. This small switch in my mental approach changed
it from "suffering" to just "being." What *is* just *is*; it's neither good
nor bad. Only our viewpoint makes something positive or
negative, just as in a war each side thinks it is made up of "the
good guys" and that the *others* are "the enemy."

By reacting to pain as a negative, and fighting it, we increase
the painfulness of it. By treating it as a fact and not reacting
to it, just letting it be there, surrendering to it as a feeling, we
let it pass through more easily. Rigidity, which comes with reaction and judgment, tends to hold instead of release. This is what
I had learned, and what I shared at our seminars.

Whenever I felt that people were not getting the gist of what
I was trying to convey, I let my enthusiasm roll into high gear,
hoping that at least some of them would sense intuitively what

they couldn't understand with their minds. "There is something wonderful in life that can't be found in the marketplace, the schoolroom or the theater!" I would say. "It is so important that if you don't have it, it doesn't matter what else you do have." In the Bible it is phrased this way: *"Seek ye the Kingdom of God; and all these things shall be added unto you."* At last some of the Bible's messages were beginning to have meaning for me and I wanted to make them alive and meaningful for others as well.

Often, people were dubious about the concepts presented in the seminars. Fortunately, we don't have to believe that geysers exist in order for them to exist, and, similarly, metaphysical wonders, intangible as they are, don't need our agreement to be real.

Initially, it takes trust to commit yourself to the pursuit of the invisible. Trust is even more powerful than faith. For example, we may have faith in the abilities of a circus tightrope walker. Our faith lets us believe that the performer on the high wire will not fall, regardless of how much he teeters and jiggles on the wire. If he were to approach us, however, and ask that one of us sit on his shoulders while he crossed the wire — *that* requires trust.

A starving man cannot have his hunger appeased by feeding him the paper menu, no matter how deliciously the items are described, no matter how tantalizing the photographs appear. In the same way, many of the people who came to our seminars were full of words and pictures, but these words and pictures did not provide enough nourishment for their trust or patience to assist them in pursuing an unseen goal. It was necessary to provide some evidence that would confirm their own ability to quench the need within them.

At seminars I decided to illustrate how we armor ourselves and prevent information from reaching us that might be valuable for our growth. A king resides in the midst of his fortress, I would explain. He is responsible for running an empire and cannot be bothered with trivia, so he protects himself from being approached with mundane matters. If we wish to see the king, first we are stopped by the gateman. If we don't get past the gateman, we can go no further. If we are permitted entry into the castle, we are then screened by the secretaries and ministers. Finally, although we may be barred from seeing the sovereign, we may be promised that our message will be delivered by one of his attendants. Our brains, like the king, are constantly bombarded with input: sounds, sights, smells. Consequently, in order to concentrate, we must have a way of filtering out most of the stimuli. This is accomplished by a process known to scientists as the reticular activating system. Laymen call it "the ego." It is conditioned by biochemical impulses from the moment we are born, and it represents programming upon which the brain operates. This programming not only creates our personality, it also creates our entire reality.

If an infant hears his mother scream at the same time that he sees a spider, for instance, the ego records that moment and from then on spiders will have a particular effect on him associated with that scream. The reticular activating system is even stimulated by nerve loops in the brain itself, so that thoughts, as well as actions, can imprint on it. Thus, the ego is like the gateman at the king's palace. It only allows the brain to see certain things. It is an effective filter: anything ego doesn't want us to see, we don't see; anything ego doesn't want us to hear, we don't hear.

The activities of the ego are necessary, but unfortunately, we sometimes think we *are* the ego. And our ego, taking as much power as it can, sometimes becomes so selective that it prevents very important information from reaching our conscious mind, thus depriving us of choices. In the seminars, I attempted to assist participants in confronting their ego, so they could choose to be the masters of their ego rather than allowing the ego to master them. One exercise that demonstrated participants' receptivity to having some ego armoring removed involved my tying a light piece of woolen yarn four feet long to form a link between two people's wrists. "This is your partner for the remainder of today," I announced. "Wherever you go, your partner will be no more than four feet away."

Not all partners were of the same gender, and one woman asked in horror, "What about when I have to use the bathroom?"

"What are you afraid of?" I responded nonchalantly. She went through all her reservations and considerations, and, in the process, discovered how groundless her fears really were. After all, what she was afraid of was having her partner see her as she really was: human. Thus, our partners became our mirrors, enabling us to see our ego patterns.

The closer we got to each other, the more similar we appeared. The seminars enabled us to focus on our similarities as members of the same species, rather than our differences within those similarities. No one fainted at the discovery, no one left the seminar in shock. Growth took place in spite of ego resistance. Belief systems fell away as do dry, scaly skins from shedding snakes. People were becoming free of old fears and conditioning, and were breathing sighs of relief.

When we know who we *really* are, there can be no more fear. Fear represents apprehension over the possibility of loss. When we realize that nothing can be taken from us, that we have nothing valuable we can lose, fear evaporates. Who we are in our essence — the "Behind all *That!*" behind our egos and our programming — is so powerful and complete that I felt any shock was worth employing if it resulted in seminar participants discovering themselves as perfect, loving beings.

As the drama of the seminars at The Living Love Center increased, they became more popular than ever. As a teacher, I never hesitated to be outrageous if I thought a lesson for growth could be learned. To demonstrate the power of the mind, I once passed a can of foul-smelling chemicals around the room. "It simply represents an odor — it's neither good nor bad," I would say. "Your mind can experience it without letting prior programming automatically trigger rejection."

The can was passed from person to person. Some people actually refused to relinquish it until they spent sufficient time savoring its unique bouquet. No one gagged or even wrinkled a nose. Einstein observed that we use only a small fraction of our brains, and leave the bulk of our potential totally untapped. Unveiling the extraordinary powers of the mind was my favorite demonstration.

We have all read about people who control their own heartbeat, stop the flow of blood from an open wound or move objects with their mind. We are taught that Jesus walked on water and healed blindness. How long can we go through life without discovering that these powers are our own birthright as human beings? Why do only an isolated few give themselves permission to unleash the secret gifts we all possess? After my own surgery, I knew how easily matter could be influenced by the mind. At workshops I hoped to at least reveal the possibilities of what all the people in the room could do if they put their minds to it.

A green nut has to be picked and pried from its shell with force. A brown, ripe nut, however, will be released from its shell with a tap. I had spent years turning brown, and the taps of Hilda, Ram Dass and Ken sent me sailing into a new reality. Since I never knew how green or brown were the nuts at the seminars, I knew it was possible that many had arrived at their time for self-realization. I never picked with a sharp object — but sometimes I used a heavy hammer for tapping.

For example, when one woman broke down in tears, sobbing that she couldn't do a certain exercise, I refused to let her crying persuade me to let her off the hook. Her pattern of crumbling whenever a task requiring concentration had to be performed had controlled her for a lifetime.

Although her sobs were so persuasive that everyone in the room wanted to rush to her side to console her, I instinctively roared, "No, that won't work!" Mustering all my abilities as an actor, I pretended to be really angry. "It's time to recognize what you're doing as a pattern that prevents you from ever succeeding. You can choose to let go of it right now!" I shouted.

Stunned participants reacted as if I were an inhuman ogre, but the woman in the hot-seat suddenly realized it was true. If everyone patted her and stroked her, the crying pattern would have been reinforced, and she knew she would again convince herself and everyone else that she was helpless. Instead, she took a deep breath and performed like a champ, surprising everyone, including herself. She chose to win, and her victory would reverberate throughout her life, affecting all areas of her future.

Before each seminar, I removed myself to a quiet place and prayed for my ego not to interfere with the presentation of the

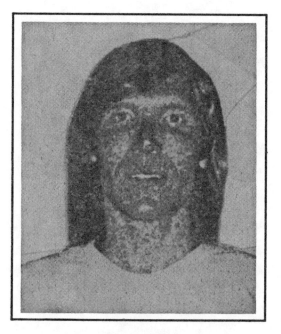

AGE TWENTY-SIX

material. I concluded my prayer with words handed down by Francis of Assisi: *"May I be an instrument of peace. Where there is hatred, let me sow love; where there is doubt, faith; where there is despair, hope; where there is darkness, light; and where there is sadness, joy. May I not so much seek to be consoled, as to console; to be understood, as to understand; to be loved, as to love. For it is in giving that we receive, it is in pardoning that we are pardoned, and it is in dying that we are born to eternal life."*

16

During the time I spent with Ken, his organization grew to the point where it was handling several hundred thousand dollars a year. I looked around and saw that other seminar groups were also attracting big money. Since I had now become a cornerstone of Ken's network and innovated many of the successful teaching techniques, a part of me began thinking that perhaps I should go off and start doing "my own thing." I'm not sure if these thoughts were catalyzed by greed or feelings of self-importance, but I surmise that both of these ingredients were present in some degree when I finally made the decision to leave Ken.

Since California was glutted with self-improvement courses, effectiveness trainings, growth seminars and human potential workshops, I decided to return to the East. Just before leaving California, I visited Ram Dass, who was staying at a house in Berkeley while he was lecturing on the West Coast. Although we had been corresponding continually, I hadn't seen him in almost a year. When I told him about my teaching work and about the physical and psychological healings I had experienced

LIVING LOVE CENTER, 1974

since last seeing him, he offered me this caution: "Don't focus so much on the virtue of attaining psychological well-being. God should be your primary concern. As spirituality unfolds, the psychological well-being just happens."

His advice helped put things into perspective as I returned to New Jersey where I founded the Organization for Sensitivity Development. The response was immediate and very positive. Doctors, lawyers, clergymen, even *psychiatrists*, flocked to my seminars.

I found it unbelievable at times to think of how close I had come to killing myself. The frenzy of youth drives so many mad, but time has an amazing power to heal the mind. If young people could only trust the healing quality in the passage of time, most would find themselves transmuted into more balanced souls capable of surviving the daily tumult. "This too shall pass" is an observation in the Kabala, the Koran, and many other philosophical and religious texts. I feel it should be repeated again and again to every suicidal person trying to escape emotional pain. When things are completely dark, it's difficult to imagine that they can get better, and it's even more difficult to realize that you don't have to do anything to make them better except to wait and be patient. "Patience" is still my most important lesson to learn, but I have been constantly growing in this area, and beg every despondent soul to wait. . . wait. . . just wait. While waiting I also recommend some type of service to others as an effective way of taking one's mind off the problem that is causing so much distress.

It was now April of 1975. Lest I give the impression that everything was totally rosy in my life since my surgery the year before, I must candidly say that it was not. There were certainly moments of self-doubt and every day was not euphoric. But although the sea of my life was frequently choppy, and, occasionally, waves pulled me under, I was buoyed by the life jacket of what I had learned, and was therefore never pulled down too far.

Two things in particular plagued me. The first was the period in which I had been so sexually promiscuous. I realized it had been a necessary part of my development as I searched for a sense of identity, but I never quite shook off the guilt I amassed from using other people for my own purposes. To remain happy, the third Life Requirement, *Self-worth*, must present itself with regularity. The memories of my sexual exploitations often kindled gross feelings of unworthiness and I would plummet from my high space and fall with a leaden thud.

The other problem I was dealing with revolved around money. Even though people were willing to pay for my seminars, and even though payment for services is the norm here in America, I was not comfortable charging money for what I did. I felt as if I was selling people something they already had. Hilda had *never* taken money, neither had Ram Dass, and though Ken generally received money for his services, he never took money from me. I was escorted along the trail of discovery without charge, and felt an obligation to pass on the teachings in the same spirit in which I received them. In my gut, I knew that true spirituality was not something to be sold like a commodity in the marketplace. To experience God is a divine gift and the exchange of money seemed to taint the purity of my efforts. Also, I remembered the phrase: *"We create our livings by what we earn, but we create our lives by what we give."* At the time I faced this dilemma, I was totally without funds, living in my parents' home again, and it had been two years since I'd performed professionally as Tolly the Clown Magician. More and more I began to be obsessed with the first Life Requirement, *Financial Security.* Confused, I telephoned Hilda for advice.

"Trust God, dear," came her sweet voice in counsel, reminding me of Jesus's words. "Look at the birds. Do they worry about food? They are fed. Look at the lilies. Do they worry about clothes? God cares for all his creation, and everything always turns out perfect in the divine scheme of things. Remember, the Lord moves in mysterious ways. Come visit me, a solution will manifest itself."

As always, Hilda bolstered my trust and I resolved to see her the following day, knowing that the mysterious ways of the Lord would be revealed. However, it was not the following day, but the same day that ended with one of the most uncanny events in my life.

I had dinner at a friend's home in Manhattan. He lived just down the street from Hilda on West End Avenue. After we ate and enjoyed our visit, I bade him goodnight and left. It was about 10:30, and there was a torrential downpour. The sidewalks and streets were slick, and I dared not run for fear of slipping. At the corner, the red "DON'T WALK" sign was lit, and I had to stand in the soaking rain. Finally, I saw the green "WALK" sign come on, and I stepped from the curb and proceeded to cross the street. Suddenly, without warning, it seemed like I was slipping back into asparagus-ness.

New York vanished. There was no rain. A silent, steady awareness witnessed my body whirling. Only three seconds passed, but they were laden with so much intensity that it will take my entire life to unravel all that I saw in those three seconds. My mind entertained countless thoughts: "I must have just died"; "Oh, no, I must have taken too many psychedelics"; "I'm having a stroke." The only thought that never occurred to me was that I had been struck from behind by a 1972 Pontiac Grand Prix, and was now spinning head over heels 25 feet in the air.

All thoughts abruptly ceased when I hit the pavement. After an indeterminate amount of time, I heard a voice somewhere in the darkness saying, "I think he's dead." Immediately, my eyes shot open. Inches above my nose, I could see the distinctive black rubber tread of an auto tire, and I knew at once I had been hit by a car. A surge of pain engulfed me, and again I lost consciousness. I recall opening my eyes once in the ambulance, but my perceptions were fuzzy. I only regained full consciousness later in the hospital.

Actually, I was quite lucky. Had I seen the approaching car before the moment of impact, my muscles would have tightened, and my stiff, rigid body would have made me a more likely candidate for total annihilation. However, because I was struck from behind, without awareness of what was happening, my body remained relaxed, sailed through the air with grace, and my life was spared. Still, the injuries I sustained seemed more than I was prepared to bear. Despite my training, my spirit was temporarily crushed. Physical pain was not localized and I found it difficult to endure; even with medication, my entire body felt as if it was being bombarded by lightning and thunder.

My bedside phone brought Hilda's consoling voice to my ear. "How are you darling?"

Her voice moved me to tears. I mumbled incoherently at first, then managed to say, "It seems like someone is shooting flashbulbs off in my eyes."

"How wonderful," Hilda exclaimed. "That's the spiritual energy coursing up your spine. It's called *Kundalini*. Be grateful that your *Kundalini* is being released. You're so lucky."

The most important lesson Hilda has ever taught me is how to create my life so that there is always a victory to celebrate. The absurdity of her congratulations turned my tears to spontaneous laughter. She cooed in my ear, and pain seemed to evaporate from me like puddles following a brief cloud-burst in the Sahara. She concluded by saying, "We'll pray for you dear," and memories of the power held by Hilda's prayers immediately soothed every cell within my broken body.

Weeks passed, and though healing was taking place, it seemed to occur in spite of the care I received at the hospital. The overworked and underpaid nurses had little time and little desire to provide what I really needed to recover. Loud voices filled the hospital corridors all during the night. Once, when my ice pack broke, no one responded to my bedside call button, and I spent the entire night shrouded in cold, wet linen. Finally, I decided I had had enough, and when some friends came to visit me on their way to Hilda's meditation class, I persuaded them to carry me out of the hospital and take me to the class with them. Ignoring the protests of nurses and physicians, I escaped into the night.

Hilda's class, which was then being held at St. Luke's Church in Greenwich Village, was already in progress when my pajama-clad body appeared at the door, supported on both sides by the arms and shoulders of my friends. I was eased into a chair, and Hilda approached. Her classes had continued to grow and about 1,000 people were present that night. Like the Red Sea, the throng of people parted before her as she advanced toward me. Nearing me, she shook her head from side to side, and emitted her wonderful laugh.

"Kids," Hilda said, addressing the crowd of young and old alike, "We must heal this child. Point your palms at Tolly and let's 'Om.' Let us call down the infinite energy of the Universe and amplify the healing power within us all. Let it come through now, kids."

Hilda placed one of her hands on my head and the other on my heart. A thousand voices created an "Om-m-m-m-m" that rumbled through the church, resounding off the walls and high ceiling. The chair in which I sat began to vibrate from the force and intensity of the tumultuous roar. In my ear I could hear Hilda's command, "Rearrange your atoms! Rearrange your atoms! Ah yes, ah yes, the atoms *are* rearranging themselves."

The "Om-m-m-m-m-m" thundered and grew louder. Hilda made no attempt to control it or draw it to a close. Minutes passed, but within me, time stood still. Colors were surging through my brain. The impact of the sound on my body made me feel as if I would collapse. Hilda sensed my inner condition and ordered me to "Hold the power. Don't let it overcome you. Contain it! Use it! Absorb it!"

The room shook as if an earthquake was unleashing the molten fury of the planet. My mind was emptied of thought as my brain swirled amid stars and galaxies. I forgot where I was, who I was, what had happened. An empty shell that once was my form disintegrated, and was blown away by the wind of the mighty Om. Only Asparagus remained. At the end of what seemed like eternity, the din subsided and I returned to my body. Hilda addressed the friends who had brought me from the hospital, instructing them to take me home and put me to bed. That night I slept as never before.

For the next several weeks, my friend Alan Cohen cared for me with tenderness and love. His home became my hospital, and healing advanced rapidly. By June, I was well enough to travel, and I flew to Florida to spend some time with my grandfather, who was living in a retirement community. I availed myself of the heated pool and health spa, swimming daily as a therapy for my recovering body. The impact of the car had caused a massive concussion, dislocated my right hip, ruptured one of my kidneys, bruised and lacerated my entire body and caused considerable damage to my spine. I felt Hilda's love with me always, and everything but my spine healed perfectly within four months. The spine would take much longer — and there were many lessons I had to learn along the way to its healing.

Disability insurance provided my income while I waited for the court to decide on a settlement. Remembering Hilda's reference to the Lord working in mysterious ways when I had phoned her for advice about *Financial Security* on the very day of my accident, I saw that for the time being, at least, I would not have to accept money for my teaching work. But now teaching itself had become a distant reality: much deep healing had to occur first.

I spent the summer with Grandpa and enjoyed the comfort of the retirement village. In the autumn, I returned to the West Coast, purchasing a small trailer which I moved to the woods outside of Columbia, a tiny town in the mountains of northern California. There, on the edge of the Stanislaus National Forest, I made my home. Without electricity or modern amenities, I sequestered myself in my little cloister and attempted to plan my future.

My mind was not clear, and bodily pain was a frequent companion. The romantic role of the hermit was the only one I felt ready to play. This image had been in my mind for years. When I had asked Valerie for a divorce, and my life was falling apart, I had imagined myself seeking refuge alone among the trees and mossy rocks. Whenever I had read novels in which there was a character who lived in a grass hut in the forest, my imagination burned with excitement. That was the character I could most easily relate to, the character I envied. I knew there was some special understanding that accompanied that way of life.

So for me, living in the woods was a dream come true — and it was not in the least disappointing. This tranquil setting soon became my long-awaited teacher in the subtle art of meditation. Neither grasping after nor pushing away, Nature and I watched the months drift by.

17

Until my car accident, I had only been concerned with my mind and my spirit. Awareness of my body and its needs was one of the more positive things that came from the accident. But like most lessons in my life, I learned it the hard way.

My spine suffered the most serious injury and was the most difficult to mend. Nerve damage and severe disc damage resulted in pain that only morphine could control. I only felt relief when my spine was either perfectly vertical or horizontal. To insure this, for months I had to wear a brace which harnessed my jaw, neck, and the back of my head and extended all the way down my back to my buttocks. When I removed the brace to wash, poor posture, such as slouching, was intolerably painful. Lounging chairs or reclining on pillows was agony. Only a wooden board with a firm foam rubber pad allowed me to sleep. There were no compromises; I had to be perfectly straight, erect or supine. I could not lie on my stomach or side and every movement required concentration.

As I explored the pains and tensions of my body, quite a lot was revealed to me about my emotions as well. My healing in the forest extended to every facet of my past. I clearly saw how much anger I harbored within me, and how many people I had yet to forgive. I discovered that it was impossible to enjoy perfect health until the body, mind and spirit were completely purged of anger. I saw that fear, too, had to be eliminated. And the forest itself provided ample opportunities to examine my fears. The mountains were alive with scorpions, black widow spiders, tarantulas and rattlesnakes, all of which had previously terrified me. But now, as I met each of these creatures, I refused to shrink away; instead I drew close to learn about them and myself in relationship to them.

In every instance, I found that they were far more frightened of me than I was of them. I researched their habits at the library, and soon they became fascinating subjects for study. Today I laugh at my acquired fear of any member of Nature's family. The first time I encountered a rattlesnake I realized that he was rattling not to threaten me or because he intended to do me harm, but simply to alert me to his presence so that he wouldn't get stepped on. I found that in dealing with poisonous creatures, all I really had to do was to learn their habits and respect them.

Life in the forest was a time of continual self-discovery. Only on rare occasions was I visited by friends, and still more infrequently would a new person hike along the trail past my hermitage, permitting me an opportunity to provide hospitality.

In my first spring there, however, when the doctors were gradually weaning me from the brace, I was visited by an old friend whose brief stay radically affected the course of my future. Her name was Linda, and I had met her through workshops at The Living Love Center. But the Linda I greeted that day in the woods outside my trailer was a very different Linda from the one I remembered.

"Linda? Is this the Linda I thought I knew?" was all I could blurt out in greeting her. My mouth was agape. There stood an attractive woman who used to have waist-length hair, but who now was as bald as a billiard ball.

"Linda?" I blinked with stupefaction. "What happened?"

"I shave my head now," was her short reply. She gave me a warm embrace and kissed me tenderly.

Her matter-of-fact response made me suddenly embarrassed, an emotion I rarely experienced. "Why?" was all I could utter.

"Well, if you ask me any question that begins with 'why', my only response can be 'because.' 'Why' questions all get the same answer. 'Because!'" And with that, the discussion seemed to be ended.

After dinner, I boldly requested, "May I rub your head, Linda?" The urge was irresistible. We both burst out laughing. She took my hand in hers and softly stroked it over her shiny pate.

"Ooh," she purred, "that feels sooo nice." We giggled and I rubbed her head again. "You'll never know all about it until you've shaved your own head," she tittered. "Wanna do it?"

"Why not?" automatically sprang from my lips.

The past three years had seen me grow my hair long — clip it; cease shaving my beard — trim it; then shave it off. Now, something new. "Why not?" I repeated, this time with conviction.

An hour later, my red hair was cast to the wind. Now it was my turn to guide Linda's hand over my own hairless scalp, and I had to agree with her: the sensation was *wonderful.*

"Shall we take a walk and watch the sunset?" I invited.

"Of course," she replied.

Arm in arm, we strolled down my favorite path, which led to an abandoned marble quarry hidden in the heart of the forest. Dozens of huge marble blocks, randomly stacked, created the impression of an ancient temple. Each stoned weighed close to ten tons, and we felt elf-like as we drew closer. The forest had long been encroaching on the temple and, as the sun set and the wind blew through the quarry, the combination of foliage and stone, shadow, light and sound, created an eerie aura of a mythological past.

"It's enchanting," Linda whispered. I nodded in agreement.

Among the stone blocks, I had previously made a bed of straw, perfectly flat so that I could lie there without hurting my spine. Often I slept in this quarry nest, but always alone. That night, the nest was full: Linda and I, and the bright, full man in the moon were a menage-a-trois, each of us beaming our shiny roundness.

The next day, Linda insisted we purchase film for her camera so that we could photograph ourselves in the quarry. Our trip into town caused more than one head to turn. Our two, cropless tops seemed to intimidate the people of Columbia, who rarely saw anything out of the ordinary in their tiny village — and we were definitely out of the ordinary.

When we stopped in a small cafe for tea, the waitress was visibly shaken, and I thought she was going to cry. How strange, I thought. When I first saw Linda, I was intrigued, certainly not frightened. Empathizing now with the waitress, I tried to understand her reaction. I sensed that she had no perception of who she really was, and totally identified with the reflection she saw each day in the mirror. Apart from that physical form, she could not imagine herself existing. She had no idea that who she *thought* she was, was not who she *really* was. The idea of altering her outward appearance as a way of learning something about her inner self was not part of her reality. Thus, she interpreted our shaven heads as an act of defiance, and she automatically labeled us as hostile. We had violated the social convention which demands that people politely blend in. Why is it so hard for people to realize how much fun it can be to be a rose of a different color? Linda and I wondered.

Linda said to her very sweetly, "Are you upset? Would you like me to explain —"

"No!" was the waitress's curt reply, and she darted away as

if pursued by demons. Her behavior gave me much to reflect upon.

That afternoon, we shot 72 photographs in the quarry. Like small children, we stripped off our clothes and frolicked among the gargantuan blocks. Linda swung from tree limbs, while I howled into the cloudless sky.

PLAYING IN THE MARBLE QUARRY

That night I shared my exhilaration with Linda. "I feel so light and airy. The removal of my hair is like the removal of some unknown weight, perhaps the weight of convention, perhaps the weight of always doing the known thing. I love it."

"Want more?" she asked.

"Sure, why not?"

That was Linda's signal, and she immediately set about gathering firewood. "Don't just stand there watching," she commanded. "Gather your share."

Soon a raging fire crackled in the crisp night air. Neither of us spoke as we watched the hefty logs being consumed by the flames. Permeated with contentment, wonder and curiosity, I observed my nimble friend as she fed the fire with more logs, weaving her mysterious web. Since my accident, I was not so ambitious to be in control, perhaps a little tired of fighting, charging through life, taking on problems, crusading and parading: it felt comfortable now for Linda to lead and me to follow.

An hour passed, maybe two. We sat in a close embrace, warmed by the dying flames. When the fire was gone, and the embers glowed red, my trance was broken by Linda rising, and snapping a branch from a nearby pine. She tossed the bough on the bed of red-hot coals and it immediately burst into flames. Without a word, she slipped off her shoes, peeled the socks from her feet, and proceeded to walk slowly across the coals.

"Linda!" I screamed.

She did not flinch but continued to put one foot in front of the other, setting it squarely down on the fiery path. I was numb. My heart pounded wildly. Was I dreaming? What the hell was this about anyway?

As she finished her walk, I suddenly blurted out, "If you can do it, I can too... can't I?" She smiled. I knew in my heart that I *could* do it, and I knew Linda would have stopped me if she thought I couldn't.

I ripped the shoes and socks from my feet and bounded onto the runway of fire. It was hot! It was very hot!! Even as my mind shrieked and rebelled at the insanity of what I was doing, my heart thrilled with exuberance, my body tingled with delight, and I knew, I *knew*, my feet would not be burned. I half-laughed and half-shouted as I finished the walk. Before my mind had a chance even to demand that I check my soles, I made an about-face, and again strode the coals. A part of me died that instant, and another part of me was born. What died was a constricting belief system, and what was born was a sense of life's limitlessness.

"How? How is this possible?" I demanded when I finally inspected my unharmed soles.

Linda, ultimately composed, said simply, "I don't know. I really don't care. What does it matter? There's no need for an explanation. It's possible and it's healthy. What else matters?"

"Linda, you're too much!" I laughed. I felt she had given me a priceless gift. For years I had crawled, then I had stumbled, finally I had learned to walk, even to run and to dance. Now she had taught me to fly. The healings I had experienced after my suicide attempts and again after the diagnosis of cancer convinced me that when the laws of science seem to be broken, it's not really a violation of scientific laws, it's that science does not yet understand all the laws of the Universe. I thought I was immune to surprise after my last healing, but walking on fire surprised me with yet another awesome discovery of the hidden power within all of us. It was a gift, indeed. I felt the exhilaration of a prisoner pardoned moments before his scheduled execution. "Thank you," I said to Linda. "Thank you for what you've taught me. I'll never forget you."

"I haven't taught you anything. You simply saw me do something, you realized that there was no difference between me and you, and *you gave yourself permission* to do the same thing. It's simple."

The next day, Linda left. She was on an odyssey of her own, which eventually led to a degree in nursing and to study with American Indian healers. Before coming to visit me, she had lived with a Tibetan Master who had shaved her head and taught her how to walk on fire. I was a stopping point for her on her way to San Francisco.

Alone once again, I busied myself with research at the library on the phenomenon of firewalking. My brain could not rest without knowing *how* it could be accomplished. Even though I had experienced miraculous healings and had survived what should have been fatal suicide attempts, my mind still needed a rational explanation of how I was able to walk unharmed on glowing coals. The library provided me with a wealth of information. I discovered that glowing coals range in temperature from 1200°F. to 2500°F., depending on the type of wood being used and the conditions under which it is burned. I also learned that molten aluminum is poured at 1100°F., and that firewalking in the Far East and in South America has caused critical injuries and death over the centuries during which it has been done.

As I continued to research firewalking, I found that over the years numerous theories, based on changes in blood pressure and laws of physics, have been presented to try to explain it. The more I read, however, the more clearly I saw that scientists and medical experts were continually contradicting each other, and most of them finally admitted that flesh should burn instantly at these temperatures.

I left my inquiry with the conviction that firewalking was still a mystery: it wasn't that Universal laws were being violated in firewalking; rather, firewalking was another example of our not yet knowing all the laws of the Universe. What I was left with was my own experience of it — an experience that I knew, from the moment I had walked across the coals, would change my entire life.

I didn't know then that future years would find me traveling all over the planet teaching classes in firewalking, nor did I have any idea that my firewalking seminars would eventually be in such demand that I would have to train dozens of others to teach firewalking, too. From my trailer in the woods I didn't have the least glimmering of a notion that the media would discover my firewalking workshops, make them world-famous, and credit me with being the first person on earth to introduce firewalking to the general public as a simple class open to all. I knew only that *I* had been changed by firewalking, that I felt freer now and more joyful and I felt deeply grateful to Linda for being the catalyst of this change.

A year came and went. I felt no desire to leave the forest. I was still experiencing pain from the accident, and I found continual nourishment in my beloved quarry temple. I was grateful for the many unexpected gifts it bestowed, gifts that I felt more and more able to appreciate. One of these gifts came in the form of music. I should explain that I had never learned to play a musical instrument. Now I was twenty-nine years old and had thoroughly convinced myself that I had absolutely no propensity or aptitude for music. I couldn't even carry a tune I thought. One sunny morning, however, as I lay sunbathing in the quarry, a song formed in my mind and would not leave. It had such a catchy tune that I couldn't get it out of my head all day. It seemed familiar, and I tried desperately to place where I had heard it before. Suddenly, it dawned upon me that I had *never* heard it; it was coming *through* me.

I began to sing it out loud. As I sang, I discovered how much I loved singing and I loved the song. I wanted to sing it over and over again. A great joy swelled in my spirit as I realized I had composed my first song. "Now," I thought, "do I dare try to learn to play it on an instrument?"

An old voice replied, "You have no musical ability. Forget it."

Then I remembered my friend, Randy Preiser, who played the guitar and harmonica, and who had once told me that every human being had the capacity to play some musical instrument. "*Every* human being," he had said emphatically. Randy felt that we sometimes stifle our musical ability because someone in our distant past may have discouraged us by ridiculing our attempts to make music. "Insignificant" events from my childhood suddenly came back to me. Every year in grammar school I had tried out for the chorus, and every year I was rejected. Finally, the music teacher accepted me out of pity, but only on the condition that I promised "not to sing too loud." Concurrent with this was my failure to keep up with the class when I attempted to learn how to play drums. All I needed to do now, I saw, was to toss out the old programming and *give myself permission* to be "musical." I had walked on fire, hadn't I?

When my Grandma was living, it was her fervent desire that someday I play the guitar. Whenever I held the instrument, however, I felt as if suddenly all my fingers were thumbs and my mind turned to stone. I was unwilling to struggle with learning to play, and it never occurred to me that it could be anything less than a struggle. Grandma was disappointed that I had never been able to play for her. Now I sensed Grandma's presence and that she was tickled with delight when I purchased a used guitar in town and brought it back to the marble quarry. A simplified do-it-yourself book instructed me in the proper finger placement. I plucked and plodded on the path of musical progress. Finally, after months of practice and experimentation, I was able to sing the song I had discovered within my self and provide my own guitar accompaniment.

The tune was slow, soft and gentle. The words were:

> When a tree falls in the forest,
> > while no one is around,
> > there is some speculation
> > as to whether there is sound.

> Well, I live in the forest,
> > I'm a solitary tree,
> > no one knows what I do here;
> > no one knows, but me.

And when I sing in the forest,
    while no one is around,
    I do not know what happens,
    but there never is a sound.

A rainbow cannot happen,
    without water, light and eyes,
    for if no one is there to see it,
    there are only endless skies.

I know I live in Heaven,
    unknown to all but me,
    singing in the forest,
    where no one else can see.

One evening, after a day spent singing in the quarry, I returned to my trailer and decided to retire early. While lying in bed waiting for sleep, a rumbling, growling sound suddenly pierced the silence of the night. It seemed close, too close. I thought it was only a few feet from the trailer but I couldn't figure out what it was. It sounded like an animal, but what kind of animal? The sound persisted and seemed to become more intense. "Could it be a bear?" I wondered. With that thought, my heart began to race, and my whole body started to perspire.

Ironically, my song started running through my brain. In a flash, I realized that I was only frightened because *I* was there to hear the strange sound. If I was not there to hear it, there would be no fear. In a second flash, my Asparagus Nature was present. The next thing I knew, day was breaking and I awoke from a restful night's sleep. A new song was composing itself in my head while I rubbed the sleep from my eyes.

> The only thing that's constant
> is the certainty of change,
> nothing ever remains the same.
>
> I knew a man who was lame,
> a year later he could run.
> The past is gone, the future has begun.
>
> After every storm, the sun comes out.
> Much of my clarity
> has grown from my doubt.
>
> Some days we are strong
> and some days we are weak.
> Sometimes we're bold and sometimes we're meek.
>
> Pleasure to pain, loss to gain,
> fame to shame,
> sun to rain.
>
> The only thing that's constant
> is the certainty of change,
> nothing ever remains the same.

I let the words explode from me as I sang out loud, filling the trailer with my new song. Still naked, I grabbed my guitar, burst through the door and ran to the quarry. There I spent the entire morning until my fingers could duplicate the tune that had been born in my mind. Though still lacking confidence as a musician, I glanced skyward and dedicated my songs to Grandma.

Nineteen seventy-seven passed, and I still rarely ventured from the forest. I meditated, composed songs, hiked in the woods, continued the slow process of healing, and gave thanks for the preciousness of it all. Now I began to understand what those phrases I had heard so much really meant — "Let go and let God," "Don't push the river," "Effort impairs the process" — they all had to do with trusting God.

The following year brought the first seeds of discontent. While a part of me felt that mountain mystics secluded in caves were among the highest souls on the planet, another part was critical of the merit of such isolation while the world condition was so pathetic. A phrase that often haunted me was, "All evil needs to flourish is for good people to do nothing."

Two schools of Buddhism address this topic. One school, known as Hinayana Buddhism, is primarily concerned with the attainment of personal enlightenment. The other, Mahayana Buddhism, is more concerned with service to humanity. These two divergent paths may be understood by imagining a seeker looking for a legendary Paradise. As the seeker treads his way through the forest or jungle, suddenly he discovers a high wall. With some struggle, he scales the wall, and on the other side, sees the long-sought Paradise. Hinayana Buddhism teaches that we descend into the Paradise and enjoy the reward of our laborious search. Mahayana Buddhism questions how much we could really enjoy Paradise knowing that our brothers and sisters are on the other side of the wall suffering, seeking and struggling. This school counsels that we go back into the world to help others find Paradise by pointing the way and helping to boost them over the wall. Only at the end of our lives may we ourselves retire to the Bliss of the Garden.

I had heard many tales that cautioned against living one's life in a retreat, since insulation from the testing world deludes us into a false sense of accomplishment. The Indian Saint, Sai Baba, whom Hilda had told me so much about, is quoted as saying that we need the abrasive sandpaper of the everyday world to rub against our egos until there are no longer rough spots. Only then can we be polished until we shine.

Many Indian stories illustrate this truth. One I particularly like tells of a yogi who spent years hidden in a cave. When he finally emerged into the world he radiated emanations of spiritual accomplishment. As soon as he approached the marketplace, however, an old man inadvertently stepped on his foot. The radiant yogi shouted a curse, and clouted the old man on his ear.

Another tale revolves around a man who withdrew from the world and studied esoteric practices until he had attained great powers. He re-entered the world boasting of his accomplishments. Finally, he announced to the king that he could be buried alive for six months and survive.

"Well, if you can do that," said the king, "I'll give you my prize stallion."

So the man was nailed into a wooden box and buried beneath six feet of earth. Shortly thereafter, war broke out and everyone promptly forgot about the buried man. The war lasted several years, and in the end, the boundary lines of the two warring nations were readjusted. As a result of this change, the site of his burial now lay in an entirely new kingdom.

Many years later, a road was being excavated and the workers unearthed a large wooden box. When the crate was opened, up sat the man. His first words were, "Where's my horse?"

Despite all his prowess in accomplishing remarkable feats of power, the man was still powerless to control his attachment to the mundane. Isolation in his retreat brought him no closer to freedom from the world's constant temptations, stresses and testing situations.

Despite the positive effects of living in the forest, I knew that it would be necessary at some point to re-enter society. I had things to share and things to learn. As this became more clear to me, I began making plans to leave my hermitage and resume life among other people.

18

After a little more than two years of living in the forest, I moved back to Berkeley and rented an apartment. Although I was no longer in a brace, I still had pain in my spine, neck, arms and shoulders, perpetual reminders of the accident that had occurred three years before. At times, the pain was so debilitating that I couldn't leave my bed. When this happened, I filled the doctor's prescription for morphine, the only medication that could give me relief. Despite the difficulty of functioning, my conscience demanded that somehow I make a positive contribution to the world of which I was a part, so I vowed to resume my teaching.

Marilyn Ferguson, in *The Aquarian Conspiracy*, describes the evolution of consciousness as having four stages. The first stage is the entry point. This entry point can be any experience or idea that suddenly challenges our entire belief system and past ways of operating. Initially, a person may become so disturbed by the input of his new experience that denial may be the only way to cope with it. However, it soon becomes hard to pretend that what really happened did not happen: one can only insist the earth is flat for a short time in the face of mounting evidence of its roundness. For many people who have been adhering rigidly to narrow viewpoints, the bursting of their bubble results in a full-blown emotional breakdown. After meeting Hilda and Ram Dass, my own state of mind, between suicide attempts, reflected exactly this difficulty at the stage of entry point.

The second stage in the growth of consciousness is a period of exploration and education. It is characterized by reading books, attending seminars, seeking teachers and making pilgrimages. Within this second stage are also many revelations that we often interpret as final enlightenment. We seem to get very high, and feel we've arrived at someplace unique. We pontificate and proselytize, frequently believing that we must save the sleepers and ignorant dullards of the world. Of course, our foolishness is seen by everyone but ourselves, until our own pomposity weighs so heavily that our feet of clay give way and we topple with a thud. Then we again forge off to explore another realm, read another book, attend another enlightenment weekend, sit at another guru's feet.

The exploration and education stage can last for years, even a lifetime. It is entirely possible never to graduate from it. However, at some point, if we are at all attentive, we begin to notice that our outer lives do not truly reflect our new beliefs and inner feelings. With that signal begins the transition into the third stage of growth, integration.

During the integration process, we begin "cleaning up our act." We start to see where there are contradictions between our actions and our words, and these contradictions gradually become unacceptable to us. For example, I believed in respecting the earth's ecology, but I never recycled my own glass and aluminum. As I became more integrated, I assumed more responsibility in this area. As I entered the stage of integration, I began to recycle at home, and when visiting friends who don't recycle, instead of leaving aluminum cans or glass bottles in their garbage, I would take them home and recycle them myself. As simple a gesture as recycling is, it's one more way I can bring my inner and outer life into alignment and feel harmonious within myself. The three R's I've learned to practice for ecological living are: *reduce* what I use; *reuse* what I can; *recycle* what I can't.

The fourth stage of consciousness growth frequently overlaps the third, just as the third overlaps the second. It involves meshing our own efforts with those of other people for the common good through "networking" or sharing resources.

After returning from my years in the woods, I was aware that it was time to move from exploration toward integration, bringing what I had learned into my everyday life. Since meditation had become such an important resource for me, and I regarded it as pure magic, I wanted to share it. As I began planning a new workshop, "the magic of the mind" seemed like the most appropriate theme. I wanted very much to pass on the lessons I had discovered since my car accident, and to report on the real magic I had witnessed in my life. The workshop would include an exercise in firewalking, I decided, giving all the participants an opportunity to discover real magic for themselves. I felt exalted and exuberant just thinking about it.

My plan materialized very quickly. My work at the Living Love Center had already given me a good reputation in the San Francisco Bay area, so the notice that I was teaching again brought many old-timers and new-comers as well. I decided that the price of admission would be determined by each person individually. On Sunday night — the last night of a three-day workshop — participants were asked to fill in a blank check with whatever amount they felt reflected the value of what they received from the weekend. In keeping with my vow to teach without charge for as long as I could afford to do so, I instructed participants to make their checks payable to the charity of their choice.

The reason I charged money at all was because of my observation that most people fail to value anything they don't have to pay for. If the objective is to encourage people to participate fully in a seminar, people must first see the seminar as a thing of value. When people pay money for something, they project at least some value upon the thing for which they are paying. The method I devised for payment reflected both my desire to teach as a service and my desire that participants make a full commitment to the work at hand.

A typical workshop began Friday night at 7:00 p.m. Although every weekend was different, we would always start in a circle, seated on cushions. Holding each other's hands, we intoned the sound of "Om" for several minutes, like separate instruments in an orchestra, contributing our own personal sounds so that from the many voices one symphony emerged, one solitary tone hovering above the center of the circle.

"We are one unit," I would say. "If we dissolve our personal identities, a new organism can be born this weekend. The whole can be greater than the sum of its parts.

"We have been trained to think in terms of separation instead of unity," I explained. "The planet itself is one unit, and the notion of separate nations is a sorry crime that allows us to believe that a disaster in one area of the globe is not the problem of people living on the other side of the planet. It's like the eyeball dissociating itself from the dilemma of the liver suffering from cancer.

"Obviously, if a nuclear explosion in one country sends radio-activity into the atmosphere, it will eventually affect the entire organism Earth — but we don't need such a major catastrophe to show us everything is connected. Already, the polluting by-products of industry in one nation are creating acid rain in countries thousands of miles away. Likewise, our reactions of anger, frustration and anxiety affect everyone with whom we come in contact and ripple out through the society and the world. Wouldn't it be better to send feelings of love, acceptance, harmony and unity rippling out into the world? World peace begins with individual people having an inner vision of peace that they wish to share with everyone on the planet."

After an introductory talk, I began the crucial task of teaching people about *Attentive Awareness*. But I did not teach this lesson with a lecture. Instead, I began with a magic show, explaining that the magician's job is to demonstrate how we limit our perceptions, and challenging workshop participants to *pay attention.*

After everyone was utterly baffled by the tricks, I violated the cardinal rule among professional magicians, revealing the gimmicks that were responsible for the illusions.

People used to attribute many ordinary events to magic, I explained. For example, a lizard would lose its tail and grow another one, and primitive people thought this was magical. However, after years of *paying attention,* "magic" was transmuted into "information" about the biological process by which the lizard grows the new tail.

Children spill milk because they aren't paying attention. Falling down a flight of stairs only occurs because of not paying attention. Car accidents, litter, even wars, all result from not paying attention. When the art of paying attention is mastered, *every* life situation presents the opportunity for learning and growth — and *every* individual then becomes his or her own teacher, because through *Attentive Awareness,* an inner guru is born to guide us along the path of optimal results.

By revealing the secret workings of magic tricks, I was demonstrating that tricks can only be accomplished because those who watch them are not paying attention. As I performed the tricks in slow motion, I would stop and say, "*Here* is where you were not paying attention." People were always surprised, yet there are many areas of our lives where we habitually don't pay attention. Frequently, we gulp a meal and don't pay attention to the flavor of the food. If we really pay attention to the taste of a raisin, our tongues have an orgasm. Indeed, if we begin to pay attention to every detail of every moment, life itself is transmuted from a mundane routine into a magical and enchanting experience. Practicing *Attentive Awareness* throughout the day becomes meditation in motion.

After an hour of magic tricks, I invited everyone outside and began to build a fire. . . a BIG fire! I explained that when the fire had burned itself to coals, we would rake them into a runway, and everyone would be given the golden opportunity to walk on the red-hot embers. Needless to say, people became quite agitated, and their reservations and considerations began to surface.

Instead of leading up to the firewalk and using it as a climax for the workshop, I introduced it immediately, so that by going through it, people could see that their beliefs — even beliefs that had been ingrained over a lifetime — could be proven false in an instant. Once they *experienced* firewalking, despite any belief they may have had about its being impossible, they could then open their minds to other new possibilities, and surrender themselves to the workshop activities that still lay ahead.

As the fire burned, we returned indoors. "No one will be forced to do anything this weekend against his or her will," I assured them. "Participation in any activity is purely voluntary."

At one of these weekends, I recall several people stating emphatically, "There's simply no way that I'm going to walk on those coals!" I asked them to write down every reason they could think of for not walking on the fire. When the lists were complete, each reason for not walking on the fire was then put on a separate piece of paper. From each of these reasons, a new list was made of new reasons that came to mind, triggered by the lead word on the paper. An hour passed quickly as people transcribed their programming and fears. I called this process "blueprinting the mind"; it was based on the observation that fear is best dissolved by direct confrontation and examination.

When the blueprinting was completed and people knew exactly what they were afraid of, I presented them with some basic information about the firewalking phenomenon. "The fire is hot, very hot, about 1300° Fahrenheit," I said. "When you step onto the coals they will feel hot. Your brain will immediately start screaming 'You're burning yourself,' but ignore it and *PAY AT-TENTION.* If you pay attention, you will notice that the heat is no more intense than walking barefoot across an asphalt street in summer. Your flesh is not being charred. The key is to not panic and disrupt the even pressure of your soles on the coals as you walk steadily along."

I continued the instructions and concluded with some comments on trust: trust in God, trust in your own inner voice, trust in me as the facilitator. After all, what kind of person would I be if I asked people to walk on fire knowing full well they would incinerate themselves?

At this particular weekend, an eight-year-old boy was among the participants. Both his parents were present as well.

"Everyone roll up your pants so they won't ignite," I cautioned. "Roll them up even if you don't think you're going to walk."

I stepped onto the runway of fire and slowly walked across it. The little boy immediately walked behind me. At the sight of an innocent child calmly walking the coals, every person present, without exception, followed suit. Without pressure, one by one they yielded to the momentum of seeing first the child and then other ordinary adults traversing the coals. Like all firewalks, it was an exciting demonstration of the power of the mind, and the energy of the group rose to a pinnacle of exhilaration.

This was just the beginning, however; things were now only getting "warmed up."

Strangers who survive a common disaster, such as a plane crash or earthquake, suddenly find themselves enjoying a camaraderie with each other that is usually reserved for family members or longtime friends. The same thing happens at a seminar that *begins* with firewalking. People are instantly willing to relate to each other in an open, intimate way. I have found no other technique as effective for making bridges between total strangers on the first night of a workshop. I know other teachers who have tried using nudity to accomplish this, but in my experience the shared depth of firewalking is far more powerful in its creation of a genuine and joyful bond.

The next day, Saturday, was a mixture of lectures, demonstrations, exercises in paying attention, sharing, touching, playing. During discussions and question-and-answer periods, the subject of using drugs such as marijuana, LSD and cocaine came up. Since participants represented a varied cross section of people, including professionals, housewives, students and even children, there was a great range in attitudes about and experiences with drugs. Some participants had used drugs extensively, and some had never even considered trying them. I told about my own personal involvement, and eventually, after a discussion in which everyone shared an opinion or experience, I put aside time for each individual to look within for his or her own answer or guidance.

I had tried every drug I had heard of that reportedly alters consciousness. My own conclusion was that useful as the drugs had been to help me to relax and expand my vision, like rafts that transport you across a river, they serve only a temporary purpose. It would be foolish to drag a raft along with you once the water had been crossed. I've always relied on the school of experience, sometimes called "the school of hard knocks," for my learning. I learned quite a bit about becoming less uptight from smoking marijuana. However, I also learned that it is a bad thing for the physical body. Our lungs were not made for smoke, and after finally smoking enough to give myself chest pains, I saw that in the long run pot smoking had become *very* harmful to my health. My conclusion was that drugs, like any medicine, may be used for a specific, temporary purpose; it is dangerous to let them become a regular routine or habit.

When the subject of sexuality arose in the workshop, I shared my complete about-face regarding my own conduct. Whereas I used to glut myself searching for more and more sexual pleasure, I now saw fidelity as the most stable and emotionally rewarding approach to sexuality and relationships. But, obviously, people have to formulate their own conclusions on an individual basis, I stressed; no one can expect to be guided by another person's advice or experience. Everyone has to do enough experimenting and reflection to form his or her own values in this area. During open discussions, I noticed that people who had adventured with promiscuity reported that they had arrived at the same conclusion as I had.

Through such candid sharing of experiences and feelings, by Saturday afternoon we had reached an even deeper level of intimacy and trust. Now the stage was set for more magic. The seven Life Requirements had been presented earlier, and it was time for people to taste something of the elusive seventh Requirement. Since my own experience of Asparagus had done more to illuminate *Constant Connectedness* than had any other experience in my life, in designing the "magic of the mind" workshop I felt it was important to devise exercises that might precipitate a similar cosmic awakening in others. The trick was to accomplish this without a car crash, or other violent or artificial means of altering consciousness!

Wilhelm Reich had discovered what ancient yogis had known for years: breathing itself links the flesh with consciousness. Controlling the breath can elevate awareness from the physical to the metaphysical. Therefore, Saturday afternoon included a breathing exercise which, when properly done, produces what I've been calling asparagus-ness or Asparagus Nature.

Lunch had been light, and by the time we began this exercise, our stomachs were empty. This was important. Everyone changed into light clothes, pajamas or simply stripped. Bedrolls were prepared as if for sleep. Participants lay on their backs, facing the ceiling. I instructed them to take a long, *deep* breath through their mouths, draw it high into their chests, and immediately release it. The process was that simple. However, the deep breathing had to continue — constantly — sometimes for several hours.

The results of this exercise are so consistent that they are entirely predictable. After ten minutes or so, the ego begins eroding our determination by whispering such thoughts as, "Why am I doing this? This is boring. I don't have to listen to what he says — I can do what I want." At this point, everyone must be reminded to "push through ego resistance. Keep breathing."

The mouth becomes dry, parched, cotton-like. "Push through it. Keep breathing."

Sometimes the hyperventilation makes the brain dizzy and the mind fearful. "Push through it. Keep breathing."

Sometimes people become upset because their body is uncomfortable, and they must be reminded to reside in their awareness of who they really are: THE WITNESS "behind all *That!*"

It has never been said that the path to enlightenment is easy. What has been said is that if it isn't arduous, it's not the right path. It has also been said that any medication that can do no harm is a placebo, and in itself can do no real good. The medicines that really heal must be used judiciously, because they can also be harmful. Wisdom dictates that intelligence and discretion govern our use of powerful healing agents.

Breathing itself is an incredible medicine because it can be so very powerful. People in the workshops were often surprised that merely through breathing in this way, their entire body could be taken over by intense sweating. But eventually the sweating subsides, as do the dryness of mouth, muscle spasms and dizziness, and a pleasant tingle begins to spread through the body.

"Keep breathing... Know who you are," I would say.

Some people began to cry, some laughed, some groaned. "Keep breathing... Know who you are."

An hour passed quickly. On the floor, bodies quivered while Consciousness with a capital "C" began worming its way out of the deep unconscious. Within the experience of each individual, a different perception was unfolding. Some were seeing colors, some were reliving memories of their distant pasts. Frequently, people curled into fetal positions and returned to an experience of infancy. The entire process is a catharsis that unfetters the mind and lightens the burden of accumulated psychological stress. Occasionally, a scream would override the sound of the breathing, not the scream of torment and pain, but the scream of ecstasy and release, the lover's climax exploding in orgasm.

Two hours passed and the group began arriving at the point of destination. One by one, participants relaxed into a peaceful sleep, floating on an ocean, empty of thoughts, empty of dreams, each experiencing a unique and personal perception of connection to the Universe, each merged with the state that exists prior to birth.

Before three hours passed, everyone had completed the process. Gentle music was switched on to rouse the group and ground them back into the reality of the room. We sat in a circle and spoke about our experiences.

"I can't believe three hours passed," one woman reported. "It seemed like only fifteen minutes."

Several heads nodded in agreement.

"A man said: "It was so hard at first; I finally saw that my ego resistance was about to cheat me again, and I just decided it was time to be the master of my life, and not let it happen. Then, before I knew it, I became a breathing machine and it continued automatically."

Again came concurring nods.

"I think this was the first time I've really experienced love," another gentleman added. "It was miraculous. This strange sensation surged through my body. It was so alien and unfamiliar. All of a sudden my chest got warm, and it felt as if my heart was four or five times its normal size. Suddenly I felt like laughing there was so much joy in me — but instead, I cried because

I realized that it was love and it was only now at age forty-five that I first discovered it."

More nods confirmed he was not alone.

Then came descriptions of each person's encounter with Asparagus Nature, their individual journey into the absence of thought. In each case, it had moved them far beyond their rational mind. It was the revelation that brought all the lessons of the day into focus: the magic, the feeling of union among us, the love, the awe, the power. Words were inadequate to convey what had happened, but because we had all been there, words were unnecessary. Everyone understood.

Dinner that night was clear broth. The workshop was not over; the evening held yet more surprises.

"There is only One. There is One Universe. . . One Mind with all our little thoughts. There is One Universal Color with many hues." I held up five fingers. "What's this?" I asked.

"Five fingers," came a reply.

"No! It's *one* hand."

Then I shared with them what I had discovered for myself: if we are to sense our immortality at all, we must discover the One of which we have always been a part, still are a part, and always will be a part. Until we comprehend the true nature of existence, we are stumbling blindly through life like cartoon characters constantly bumping into obstacles and falling into mud puddles. Everything in the Universe is connected and we are a part of THAT. *Never at any time are we separate from the Source of creation.* This insight is basic to progress on the path of understanding. Our separateness is an illusion. We are One with Creation — One with the Creator. The Creator listens to the birds through *our* ears and sees the sunset through *our* eyes. We are the organs of sense which enable God to witness His creation and participate in its unfolding.

Always being in contact with this sense of Oneness is the blessing of attaining the seventh Life Requirement: *Constant Connectedness.* When this aspect of our nature is finally cultivated, we are liberated forever and perfect understanding allows us to go through life as masters of our own destinies. Few human beings ever achieve this. I wanted to come up with an exercise to assist us all in glimpsing this magical place, because, more than anything else, I wanted to be a catalyst for people's growth, and I felt even a moment of *Constant Connectedness* could be transformational.

I constantly prayed: "*Use* me Lord. Show me how to best serve and help people grow." Consequently, some unusual and radical growth procedures were revealed to me. Some things, like the firewalk, were a challenge to introduce. Since no one else I knew was using such extreme techniques in the context of a seminar, there was no one to whom I could turn for advice or guidance other than my own inner Self.

In assisting people toward *Constant Connectedness*, my inner sense told me it was very important for them to overcome any aversion to being touched by others. I felt it would be beneficial to earnest seekers of truth to push past their boundaries so they could experience physically merging with other human beings in a non-sexual way. Usually, only sexual intercourse allows us to merge so fully with someone else.

The American Indians have a sacred ritual that is performed in a sweat lodge. The sweat lodge is a dome with a low ceiling and a narrow diameter. Within this tiny, darkened space, as many as fifteen people huddle close together in the blackness. The intensity of the squeeze dissolves any awareness of where your own body ends and the next person's begins. One breathing, sweating body of flesh seems to result from so many bodies being pressed together. The physical unity greatly enhances whatever ritual is performed within the sweat lodge. In longer workshops, I have had participants construct such a lodge, but during these weekends, I had an alternative way of helping us all get at least a sense of *Constant Connectedness*.

The exercise affected people profoundly. It also required a profound commitment on their parts to force themselves to go beyond their previous barriers — deep, lifelong fears that restricted them in every aspect of their lives. The ability to make this commitment to "push through" was supported by the nurturing environment of the workshop. It was also supported by the trust participants had developed in me to be working with them to serve their growth process, so that they could more fully realize themselves as joyful, feeling beings, contributing parts of a greater Cosmic Whole.

Late Saturday night, we removed our clothes and entered a room so tiny we had to squeeze extremely close to each other to fit in. There was enough air, but there was no light — and not enough space to change the position of your body once everyone had gotten in.

"For the next hour we will Om. Om with the passion and intensity of a lost child crying for its mother."

Those were the only instructions I gave.

The Om began. It swelled and enveloped us. It changed constantly: sometimes soft, sometimes loud, but always there. Soon, the heat of our bodies released the sweat that dissolved our barriers of skin. It was impossible to determine where your body ended and your neighbor's began. Suddenly we really were melted into one. No one could move. Even the slick slime of perspiration was not sufficient to lubricate a descent to the floor if someone was inclined to faint in the claustrophobic containment of the closet.

The Om became a roar. In the midst of it could be heard an occasional scream, a whimper, a laugh. And "behind all *That!*" here *we* were: silent observers witnessing whatever swirled before us in the blackness.

The hour concluded, and a puddle of people devoid of their egos poured from the tiny room.

No one spoke. No one could. Saturday was over. "Sleep well," I announced. "I'll wake you at seven in the morning."

Sunday found the group transformed. People were relating without personalities: ideas and feelings were being communicated without the colorations usually injected by our ego's pattern of declaring our individual identities. People no longer saw themselves as separate from each other. There was a peace in the room that few had ever known before.

I began the day by telling some incidents from my life. I focused primarily on the electric shock treatments, insulin coma therapy, surgical anesthetization and all the other experiences that had stripped me of the common consciousness we use to walk though each day.

"There is a tunnel we must all pass through," I would say. "Most people only enter it at the end of their lives, and they call it 'death.' The tunnel is very narrow and there is only one thing you can take through. When I first entered this tunnel after attempting suicide, when my heart had ceased to pump, I remember a speck of a hole through which I had to squeeze at the far end of that tunnel. Everything had to be left behind, except for one precious possession... *awareness.* It is important to disidentify one's Self from all the outer trappings. None of that came into the world with you."

We don't realize the strain that we place on ourselves in our daily lives because we identify so totally with our external — temporary — reality. As an exercise in dissociating ourselves from our own exteriors, I suggested that we see what it's like to let go of any attachment we might have to our personal forms. As I spoke about disidentifying with appearances and identifying only with that which could pass through the narrow tunnel, I picked up a pair of scissors and clipped huge chunks of hair from my scalp, allowing them to fall to the floor. I then produced a razor, and, sharing again what I had learned with Linda, explained that I would shave my head to illustrate a willingness to let go of familiar pictures of who I might think I really am. An invitation was extended to all present to join me in the procedure.

As we sat in a circle, the scissors were passed from one person to the next. If someone elected to have his or her head shaved, the shears were used first to remove the bulk of hair, but not before the person told the group the reason for choosing this. Those who chose not to shave their heads had only to say "No" and pass the scissors to the next person in the circle.

It is interesting to note that at some weekends, all the people risked walking on fire while at the same gathering only half decided to shave their heads. It is ironic that people were more willing to face the risk of enduring physical pain than to allow

possible injury to their ego. That statement in itself reveals so very much about human nature. Another interesting fact is that, generally speaking, women choosing to have their heads shaved outnumbered men three to one.

In giving their reasons for having their heads shaved, many people cited their desire to complete the past and begin anew. Others felt it would align them with a spiritual tradition that goes back thousands of years, and that this alignment would help them to focus on their own spiritual nature. Sometimes, people said they were not sure why they were doing it, but that they knew instinctively that it would result in growth. Frequently, women said they wanted people to see who they really were.

After the head shaving was completed and we had finished lunch, we gathered for another act of magic. I had set up a huge altar upon which pictures of some of the world's greatest saints had been propped. Candles were lit, incense kindled, flowers arranged, and soft music played through stereo speakers. What could not be seen by anyone in the group was that behind the altar was a four-foot-by-seven-foot mirror.

The group was instructed in the singing of a devotional chant which praised the Almighty and opened our hearts to the feelings of overpowering love. Our clothes were removed, and we faced the altar as we sang. One at a time, I took each person by the hand and led him or her behind the altar.

"It's time to meet your guru," I whispered, seating the person on a huge purple pillow in front of the hidden mirror.

The purple pillow was surrounded by garlands of flowers, colorful fruit, candles and incense. None of this was visible from where the other workshop participants sat. All they could see were the shoulders and head of the person behind the altar. Thus, none of the uninitiated knew what to expect.

Once seated on the purple pillow, as promised, people did get to meet their true guru: they saw themselves reflected naked in the mirror. They could also see all the other people looking at them. . . eyes filled with love, voices singing their glory. Few remained dry-eyed. As each person saw his or her own beauty, and the impact of *who* they were struck them squarely, tears flowed like dams spilling winter run-off. For me, it was the most rewarding part of the weekend.

As Sunday moved into the late afternoon, people sensed that the journey would soon be over. They had come together only two days before as total strangers, and now they were closer to one another than they were to many people they had known for years. Gone were facial lines of anxiety and stress; people looked years younger than they had when they had first arrived.

Although every seminar was different, one element they all

contained was an appeal to each person present to go out into the world to perform some act of service. To illustrate how easy it is to give, I asked everyone to sit in a circle. Every other person was then requested to get up and form a second circle within the original circle, so that those in the inner circle faced those in the outer circle.

A kettle of warm water was placed at the hub of the ring and everyone sitting in the inner circle was given a sponge. The instructions were simply, "Look into the eyes of the person in the outer circle, say 'please serve me by allowing me to serve you,' then moisten the sponge and wash the person's feet. When you are finished, kiss the feet and move on to the next person, repeating the sequence until you've washed every person's feet."

Upon the completion of this process, which took considerable time, we gathered to share what we had experienced. Without

AGE TWENTY-EIGHT

exception, people always revealed that it was easier to give than to receive.

The workshop concluded with each person pledging to perform a meaningful service in the community in which he or she resided, and specifying to the group exactly what that service would be. I encouraged people to make use of their innate talents and skills so that the form of service would be an effortless extension of their being. Checks were then written to charities as payment for the seminar, and another weekend that could have been mundane had instead become a "magic show."

19

For the next two years, I continued to give workshops in Berkeley and expanded my network to include the rest of California. It was a rewarding time for me. Although only a few years before I had had constant thoughts of suicide, it seemed that once I decided to live, everything fell neatly into place — everything, that is, except for the persistent pain from my spinal injuries. I could go for three weeks without any symptoms, then I would wake up in such agony that I couldn't leave my bed for five days. I spent a great deal of time visiting doctors and they all told me the same thing: several discs in my cervical spine had been ruptured, and since it was impossible for them to heal, they would have to be removed surgically. But no doctor would guarantee that even after surgery I would be free from pain.

I was confused about what to do. Sometimes I felt that with such a dismal prognosis, it would be better to live with the pain than risk "going under the knife." I also knew from my prior experiences that healing was possible without surgery — but I was starting to lose patience. When I looked within for some guidance, not one, not two, but a thousand voices shouted out conflicting advice. One voice would say, "Listen to me," and another would shout, "Don't be fooled, that's your ego, listen to *me!*" Still another would assert, "*I'm* the right voice, follow what *I* say." Soon I'd become more confused than ever.

For years I had been convinced that inner guidance is always available, yet because I never succeeded in clearly connecting with it, I now began allowing doubt to erode my confidence in its existence. Through prayer, I entreated the Almighty to grace me with this gift. Shortly thereafter, I had my first experience of "the pink lightning bolt."

One morning I was feeling extremely happy. I remarked to myself that if every moment of my life was spent in this state, it would be sheer bliss. I couldn't imagine feeling any more perfect. Just at the moment I thought this, a bright flash of pink lightning bolted through my brain just behind my forehead. I saw this pink lightning bolt as vividly as if it had been an image on a color television screen inside my skull.

Although this experience stirred my curiosity, soon I forgot about it. Later that same day, I fell into a depression. Tremendous sorrow weighed on me as some dark memory that I could not identify clouded my high spirits. Suddenly I became aware of another distinct image on the television screen in my head. I saw what appeared to be a golf ball with black worms wriggling in and out of it. It was a peculiar image, distinct and cartoon-like.

Ever since that day, I've noticed the pink lightning bolt when I'm experiencing a very positive frame of mind, while my negativity always produces the golf ball with the black worms. Seeing this correlation, I began using the pink lightning bolt as a guide. When an important decision has to be made, I merely look up into my forehead and wait for the non-verbal sign. If the golf ball with worms appears, it is a negative signal; if the pink lightning bolt appears, it is a positive signal. I have never been betrayed by this technique, which I regard as a genuine rapport with the Source of my creation. It guides me in a manner that has added to my sense of well-being and given me confidence and strength in all my endeavors.

I first used the pink lightning bolt technique in dealing with the question of my surgery. Every time I thought of having an operation, I would look into my forehead for guidance — and I would see the golf ball with worms. After consistently receiving this signal, I felt comfortable with the decision not to have the suggested operation.

When I saw how helpful the pink lightning bolt method was for me, and how much easier it made my life, I began to include it in my workshops. There, everyone discovered that they could connect with their own form of guidance. For some, it was a visual image: a face, a color, an external sign — maybe a bird flying overhead at just the right moment. For others, it was an inner-voice verbalizing a specific message or a printed word leaping from a page or relaxation flowing through their bodies when they thought about one course of action as opposed to another. I shared what my own experience had been, observing that if you persistently ask for a sign, it will be given.

I found it important to focus on these techniques at the beginning of a seminar, so that participants would begin to develop their own means of verifying within themselves whether a particular exercise was correct for them. I requested that every person accept full responsibility for any benefit he or she received from the weekend — which meant that none of them should follow my instructions blindly. Getting in touch with my own inner guidance helped me to respect other people's as well, and I encouraged workshop participants to connect themselves to this, their most valuable resource. If they did so they would not really be surrendering to me as a teacher, they would be trusting their own inner guidance and surrendering to that.

There is an old Sufi tale that tells of the Devil approaching a talented man and telling him he is wasting his gifts by not helping suffering humanity. "You are so capable," the Devil counsels, "it is your duty to share your wisdom." Then the Devil recommends that the man tout his qualifications so that people will believe the services he is providing are that much more valuable. Before long, the Devil creates a self-centered egotist who becomes deluded with illusions of self-importance. Soon, the man is traveling about thinking he is doing Godly service, but is really mired in a quest for recognition and fame.

Having already experienced the trickiness of my own ego, sometimes I had qualms about teaching others. Once I realized that people only teach themselves it made me feel easier.

"I still have an ego," I would remind members of the seminar, "and though I'll do my best, I know my ego can get in the way and prevent me from being a channel for higher wisdom. Ultimately, your own inner guidance is your only true teacher."

Since learning is really a process of getting in touch with something we already know deep inside, once we discover our inner guide, anyone or anything can catalyze learning. Therefore, a teacher is really only a catalyst — but we don't always need a teacher in order to learn. Often, things just need to be connected in a certain way — by something we hear or something we see — and our inner wisdom begins to flow.

For me, the continuing pain resulting from my car accident was a great teacher. Not only did it help me to get in touch with my inner guide, and the *certainty* that there is an inner guide in everyone, the pain also served as a reminder of how well off I was despite it. I had been taught by Ken that every experience that wasn't enjoyable could be used for growth, and as I looked at the pain in my spine, I was constantly faced with the question, How many people were there who would have gladly traded their afflictions for mine? It didn't take great attentiveness to see that there were others whose crosses were far greater to bear than my own. So it wasn't with a sense of injustice, but rather with a sense of victory, that I resolved to put the pain in perspective and continue teaching.

More and more, I could see there were times I had been giving pain too much power over my life. On occasion, the pain was localized enough for me to have used *Attentive Awareness* to merge with it, so that I would not feel it as such an intruder in my body, but it would have taken so much concentration to do this that I would have been unable to do anything else. Because there were so many things I wanted to do, I decided to use another approach: I resolved to become so much bigger than the pain that it would become miniscule in the vastness of my new being. To do this, I used *Attentive Awareness* to distance myself from it, to help me see that *I* wasn't the pain — the pain was only a particle contained within my infinite awareness. Simply by being willing to live with the pain regardless of its intensity, it became increasingly manageable.

I had heard a story that made a great impression on me. It was about three men who receive gifts from God. The first man uses his gift selfishly, for his own gain. The second man uses his gift to exploit others, and causes harm. The third man is fearful of losing his gift or having it stolen, so he buries it for safekeeping. Some time later, God decides to see what these men have chosen to do with their gifts. When He sees that the first man is using his gift selfishly, He is disappointed. When He sees that the second man is causing harm with his gift, He is even more disappointed. When He sees that the third man isn't even using his gift, He takes it back. Most simply put, the moral of the story is, "If you don't use it, you'll lose it."

When I thought about myself in relation to this story I realized that over the past few years, despite my teaching, I had buried many of my gifts. Feeling that the purpose of my life was to share as much as possible, I wanted to dig up these gifts to channel them into community service. I again started making regular visits to local hospitals as a clown magician. Dressed in full costume and wearing a red wig, I would spend several hours stopping in each room to perform a five-minute magic show. Besides bringing joy to the patients, this work brought a great deal of joy to me, too. Again I experienced the fundamental truth of *Active Compassion:* that when you serve others, you are also serving yourself. As a teenager I had done the same work, but it had grown more out of my need to compensate for my low self-esteem; now it was an extension of a deep feeling of *Self-worth.* Thus, I was able to do more than just entertain in the hospitals: doctors, nurses and patients often would tell me that my work had become a healing ministry, and I was frequently brought into the intensive care unit to visit some of the most critically ill patients.

TOLLY THE CLOWN MAGICIAN

I found other ways to serve as well. I began reading several times a week to an 80-year-old blind man who lived down the street and helping another neighbor, who had recently been widowed, by driving her to the market to do her shopping. I also met a very likable 84-year-old woman who had been confined to a wheelchair in a hospital for ten years. Learning that she had never been outside in all that time, I began taking her on outings whenever I had a chance. Another activity from my youth that I now revived was working with the Boy Scouts. As an Eagle Scout, I had many skills to share in our local scout troop. It was surprisingly easy to do these things, and the joy they produced both in others and myself more than compensated for the little effort they required.

Recently, there has been a rise in the popularity of another form of service with which I also became involved while I lived in Berkeley: the Cardio Pulmonary Resuscitation (CPR) education movement. I found out about it one night when my friend Tony Cantea was visiting me in my apartment and I tried to swallow some large vitamin tablets. As the tablets started their descent, one of them lodged in my windpipe and I began to choke. I'd often heard of people choking to death, but I'd never seen or experienced more than a simple misswallow that could easily be cleared by a cough. Suddenly, I couldn't breathe. I couldn't even talk. I tried to speak, but it was impossible. I grabbed my throat and started pounding my chest, but I still could not breathe. All at once, I realized the direness of the situation.

Tony asked, "Are you choking?"

I couldn't answer.

He repeated, "Are you choking?"

I nodded desperately.

Immediately, he stood behind me and folded his arms around my diaphragm and performed a rescue reflex that compressed my upper cavity. No results. He performed the maneuver a second time and the tablets shot from my mouth like bullets. When I asked him where he learned the technique, Tony told me it was part of a free CPR class given at his local fire department. The following day, I inquired to see if there was a CPR class offered in my community, and when I found out there was, I enrolled in the next course. Once I learned the CPR technique, including the Heimlich maneuver that my friend had used on me, I realized that anyone, even children, could learn these simple methods for saving lives, and that people who are equipped with this knowledge are great resources to their families, friends and communities. I passed this information on to the people in my workshops. I also called my parents, my brother Barry, and my friends, and soon they were all studying CPR.

When I looked only at the discouraging conditions in the world, I often felt overwhelmed and helpless to alter things. The more I committed myself to service, however, the more I saw that I didn't have to be paralyzed by viewing the overall picture. I needed only to look at the small corner of the community in which I lived to see immediately where I could make a difference. As soon as I began doing this work around my home base, I felt united with the leaderless network of people who are committed to service all over the world — and I realized that this service, taken *in toto*, produces a global effect.

Too often I had complained about what was wrong with the world, with our leaders and our communities. But I never saw that I, myself, possessed a solution. If I truly desired a better environment in which to live and eventually to raise a family, I had to stop criticizing and start doing what was necessary to bring about a better quality of life for myself and my neighbors. Judging from the results of my own work in community service, I could see that the more people there are who concern themselves with ordering, harmonizing and cleansing the area in which they live, the sooner the entire world community will be transformed. I could even see how overcrowded cities did not have to be such a blight: if they were filled with people *serving* one another, they would be a paradise!

The more I immersed myself in service, the more I felt I had discovered a secret that was transforming my entire life, ensuring that I would always be free and never lonely, always receiving an abundance of whatever my heart desired. As I continued to grow in consciousness, I also grew in my awareness of other people's feelings and needs. This helped me progress toward another goal I set for myself: never to take more than I was giving and never to take more than I needed.

I had learned that the problem with our country's economy was that we consume more than we produce; I was constantly on the alert to make certain that I didn't fall into this same deadly pattern. I felt that consuming more than we produce was a basic cause of stress. As I began to use less, I felt better knowing that there was that much more for everyone else to share. The greatest problem on earth today is that 80% of the world's resources are consumed by 20% of the world's population. In addition to its economic impact, such an imbalance clearly has an effect on the stress level of the entire world.

In my workshops, I began to put a greater emphasis on the remarkable value of service. When people told me they were isolated or friendless, I was not surprised to find out how much time they spent in front of a television set, playing with electronic toys or simply drinking. When illness, divorce or any life change struck one of these people, they felt they had nowhere to turn. I would encourage everyone in my workshops not to spend so much time alone, and to become a volunteer in at least one community service organization.

When people asked what they could do if they only had a limited amount of time, I suggested that any outflow of service would make a difference, regardless of how modest it was. Caring for an ailing neighbor, watching a friend's children on an evening or a weekend so that she could go shopping, visiting a shut-in or simply picking some litter up from the park are all immeasurably helpful. Just learning CPR so that it is ready to use in an emergency is a significant contribution. The possibilities for service are limitless, I've discovered; only imagination is necessary to find them.

Four years had passed since my car accident, and, in spite of the pain in my spine, I was able to enjoy many of the seven Life Requirements. One area of my emotional life where I sometimes felt frustrated was in the relationship I was having with a woman named Norma. I had known Norma since 1973 and we had been involved with varying degrees of intimacy ever since. We were friends; we were lovers. She was the only person I knew who would share my delight in putting on a full clown costume and face to go shopping, knowing that it brightened the day of everyone who saw us. On a moment's notice, she would hop on an airplane to meet me in a city a thousand miles away, while I was doing a workshop, just so we could drive back together. When my pain was so unbearable that I had to stay in bed, it was Norma who took care of me. She was intelligent, sophisticated, beautiful, compassionate, spiritual, sensual, and twenty-five years older than I was.

Since I had returned to Berkeley, we had become more and more romantically entwined. I proposed to her several times that year — and always received the same answer. "Tolly, I won't let you marry someone older than your mother."

Frustrating as this was, my love for her never diminished, and I resigned myself to enjoying the relationship without marriage. When I consulted my inner guidance about the prospect of Norma changing her mind, I didn't see the pink lightning bolt, much as I wanted to, but I did hear a voice that told me, "Don't worry. Your mate is on her way."

20

One morning, when the pain in my spine was so disabling that it was all but impossible for me to get out of bed, a special delivery letter arrived from my brother, Barry. Hilda was returning to India for the first time in nine years, he wrote, and I was invited to come along. The object of the trip was to visit Hilda's teacher, Sai Baba. Reading this name immediately brought to mind all the stories I had heard about his ability to materialize objects from the air and heal every infirmity imaginable.

When I was younger, I was constantly looking for what I could get out of life. As time made me wiser, I became more concerned about taking less for myself and giving more to others. Even though the pain from my spinal injuries was usually manageable, it still stopped me from accomplishing all that I wanted to accomplish. On reading about the trip to India, I found myself hoping that Sai Baba could relieve this pain both because it would benefit me directly, and also because it would free my energy to serve others better.

Later that afternoon, when Norma called, I asked her if she

would like to go to India with me, but she said, "No, no, Tolly dear, you go alone and maybe you'll meet a younger woman whom you can marry." Having learned not to try to change Norma's mind, I proceeded to make plans for the journey. Fortunately, my schedule was open, and within the next two weeks I was able to get a passport, all the necessary visas and innoculations, and join Hilda in New York.

The trip to India was a true pilgrimage, spanning almost three months. Fifteen students accompanied Hilda, some planning to leave early to honor work commitments, others joining later for the same reason. We first went to Greece, then Egypt, Jerusalem and Sri Lanka. The reason for visiting Greece was Hilda's conviction that one of her prior lives had been spent there as Espasia, consort to Pericles. Pericles is known as "the father of democracy," and Hilda attributed his political innovations to his having attained enlightenment. Since I had never been to Greece, I was delighted to make the trip, though I was skeptical about her reference to being reincarnated.

As we traveled, Hilda would stop at the ruins of ancient temples, and sit us down to meditate. She explained that the crumbling stones still possessed the power that ancient rites and rituals had invested in them. They were analogous to batteries, she said; the vibrations of the prayers and chants, as well as the energy focused on the place by thousands of minds now long gone, were still locked within the stone. She referred to these old temples and altars as "power centers," and encouraged us to be sensitive to the power emanating from them while we meditated.

I was on this journey to learn and grow. Therefore, I set aside my beliefs and judgments, making myself as receptive as possible to whatever might arise. My mind was able to relax, and I was generally able to surrender my ego as I followed Hilda with my heart.

When we arrived at the Acropolis, hub of the ancient Greek Empire, we were told that the Parthenon was closed to tourists.

It had been subjected to too much wear, and was not considered structurally safe enough for the public. Since guards were strategically posted to keep people out, we gathered at one end of the temple, and surveyed it as best we could. Suddenly, one of the guards looked at Hilda and hurriedly came over. He sheepishly took her hand, bowed his head and said, "Espasia," pronouncing the name with the Greek pronunciation, "Es-pa-see-a," which we had never heard before.

We all fell silent and Hilda, like the queen she was, closed her eyes and smiled. When she opened her eyes, the guard, still holding her hand, led her up the temple steps, and walked her into the center of the towering Parthenon. Since hundreds of tourists were swarming about, forbidden to enter the temple, this display caused quite a number of heads to turn. With an audience of spectators looking on, the guard slowly took Hilda to all corners of the mammoth white marble structure, and then returned her to us.

Since neither he nor Hilda spoke the other's language, the entire scene transpired in silence. When he finally let go of her hand, Hilda bent down and touched the man's feet saying only, "Thank you." It was a very moving moment, and for me, a stunning lesson in humility. I couldn't even begin to comprehend what had just happened; even if Hilda *was* Espasia, who was the guard?

After Greece, we visited Cairo. Hilda wanted to pray for peace in both Egypt and Israel. Because the tensions of the Middle East were a long-standing stress for the entire planet, Hilda felt compelled to do her healing work in this sector of the globe. When the travel agent was casually informed of the purpose for our trip to Egypt, he refused to accept money for Hilda's fare from Athens to Cairo. "I will pay for her," he said. "That will be my contribution."

The devotion and sincerity of Hilda's demeanor in the Great Pyramid, and again at the Wailing Wall of Solomon's Temple, are vividly and indelibly impressed in my mind. The sweetness and power of her prayers seemed to hold the fate of the world in balance. After our return to America, when Egypt and Israel finally agreed to a peace accord, all of us in Hilda's group felt a special reward for our efforts in behalf of world peace.

We kept a grueling pace. Because of flight schedules, we often went to sleep as late as three in the morning, and had to arise two hours later at five. It was remarkable to see how fresh and vital Hilda was in contrast to the rest of us who were perhaps fifty years younger and always dragging behind her. Her diet was usually tea, cookies and toast, yet she was nourished by some invisible energy that constantly rejuvenated her. I was so exhausted by her pace, I often felt tempted to leave and fly directly to India.

In Sri Lanka, we spent one scorchingly hot afternoon at a zoo. As we gathered around the bear pit, I tried to stir the sleeping bears by shouting at them. My shouts echoed and resounded from the concrete walls, but the bears, subdued by the heat, did not budge.

Hilda looked into the pit at the furry heaps and pointed to the largest. "Watch this," she whispered. In a voice barely audible, she began repeating, "Jambavat, Jambavat, Jambavat," addressing the largest mound of fur. After Hilda had whispered this mysterious incantation perhaps five or six times, the huge bear shot up as if he had been jolted from sleep by a flaming arrow. He stood erect on his hind feet and reached up toward Hilda with huge extended paws. Suddenly, he let forth a growl that reverberated and enveloped the entire zoo. We all laughed, but Hilda gazed at him silently, radiating the love that shines on a mother's face as she nurses her child.

As we continued our tour of the zoo, we could see, in hindsight, that it would have been better to have arrived there in the morning, when it was less hot, and the animals had more energy. At this point in the afternoon it seemed they were all taking a siesta. When we came to the lions' lair, we found a few of the mighty beasts sleeping on the ground. The rest were hidden from our view, enjoying the shade of a cement cave. Several of us tried to wake the cats by shouting and tossing popcorn. They were oblivious to our presence, however, and not a tawny muscle flinched.

Hilda smiled and softly whispered, "Durga, Durga, Durga." She made a flourish with her hand, and instantly *all* the lions sprang to their feet, roaring. Simultaneously, from the cavernous hole that hid the rest of the cats from view, a rumble of roars suddenly thundered out, startling us with its intensity. Hilda laughed and said, "Oh, no, that's too much power." She waved her other hand and the sound stopped. All the lions in the pit rolled over, and were immediately asleep again.

I was constantly disoriented by this unusual woman. Since she refused to conform to my ideas of what an enlightened being would be like, I never fully understood her. I thought that enlightenment was an egoless state, and questioned her use of hair dye and makeup. At times, I perceived her as eccentric; at other times, almost ordinary. When extraordinary things happened around her, as they constantly did on this trip, I found myself trying to rationalize them as coincidental. After all, how was I to deal with someone like Hilda, given the fact that I had never met anyone even remotely like her before? Because I had such easy access to her, it was impossible for me to conceive that she might be one of those remarkable people who are referred to as Masters and Saints. Occasionally she seemed self-centered; more often, the exact opposite. Once, when I asked her about these contradictory perceptions, she just laughed and said, "Self-centered, hmmmmm, well, after all, I love Hilda, too."

Traveling together, I was spending more time in her company than I ever had before, and I found that there were no categories into which she fit. Gradually, I resigned myself to accepting and trusting her, even though it seemed that I would never understand her.

Before leaving Sri Lanka, we made a two-day journey into the jungle. Our destination was the Sacred Temple of Kataragama, site of the altar to the Hindu god, Skanda. This temple is the holiest of the holy temples in Sri Lanka. It is the only Buddhist temple in the world where Hindu gods are worshipped. What makes this even more unusual is that Buddhists never worship gods at all.

To say that what I saw and experienced at Kataragama was incredible is the truth. As I've since discovered, scientists and journalists from all over the world have documented the phenomenon of Kataragama without being able to explain it. Long before scientists and journalists began their visits, however, when Kataragama could only be reached by traveling on a long, dangerous and rugged trail through the jungle, Hilda had made frequent trips there during the nineteen years of her spiritual study in the East. She explained that pilgrims journey to Kataragama to burn off old *karma*, *karma* being the Eastern law that every action in life must necessarily have a reaction. Believing that physical hardship must produce a balancing energy in the form of a reward, many pilgrims to Kataragama suffer their flesh to torture by piercing themselves with spikes or hanging several days from a steel hook that punctures their shoulders, penetrating clear through to the other side, leaving them dangling mid-air from a rope.

I could not imagine any deed being so bad that such extreme penance would be desirable. Remembering what I saw there still fills me with awe and makes me shudder. Even if mortification of the flesh does reverse *karma*, as it is claimed, thereby preventing a bad reaction in one's present life as a consequence of some former wrongdoing, I still thought it was a classic case of the cure being worse than the disease. It might even be called the Eastern equivalent of Western medicine's electric shock "therapy." The intriguing thing was that the people who were spiked and hooked showed all the signs of being transcendently happy. There was no blood, and no indication that they were experiencing pain.

Before we were allowed into the temple, attendants ordered us to bathe in the Holy River. Following the bathing, we were instructed to purchase coconuts to bring with us to the temple. At the entrance to the temple grounds, as a condition of entry, each person must smash open a coconut on a massive rock that has been placed there for that purpose. The coconut symbolizes the head, and this gesture represents a person's willingness to surrender to the rituals performed within the inner sanctum. It demonstrates that the ego is willing to die.

Within the courtyard of Kataragama, several temples housed different rites. Meekly, I entered one of the temples. A steady stream of people poured in behind me. An elephant was being led to an altar. As soon as it arrived at the altar, loud bells began to hammer. The intensity of the sound was unendurable; it was easily a hundred times greater than the clang of any large steeple bell I had ever heard. The din was monumental. It made me feel miniscule and insignificant, like an ant on Mount Everest.

My head seemed to be swelling with pressure and pain. I wanted to flee, but the crush of people constantly pressing inward made any movement impossible. I felt faint, but there was no space in which to fall. Although I had so often participated in my workshops in the exercise in which we all crowded into a small space, this experience was infinitely more intense. Squeezed upright, I suddenly felt an urge to scream, but instead I cried. Around me were dark-skinned Buddhists, eyes rolled back in bliss with only whites showing, ecstasy lighting their faces. Again I felt the urge to scream; this time, however, I became Asparagus.

My insight into this mysterious state took a great leap forward that day at Kataragama. Before, I had sensed that it was related to *Constant Connectedness*, which allows the person who is experiencing it to feel connected to everything in the Universe, and to perceive particles of energy where others see matter. Yet, when I was in the state of asparagus-ness, I felt as if I was out of my body. It never occurred to me that it was possible to function in that state. But Kataragama catalyzed an interesting graduation of Asparagus Nature into another state in which it was clear that I could function.

The shift to asparagus-ness occurred when I felt I was about to scream in reaction to the piercing bells. Once I was in this state, however, I no longer felt like screaming because I now experienced everything as benign, and I could no longer hear the bells. In the past, I would "awake" from this altered consciousness, and things would appear to be the same as they had been before I had "left"; this time, Asparagus Nature lasted for several minutes, and then it began to fragment. Each fragment took a different shape and color, and soon Asparagus was replaced by Paisley: alive, moving, abstract images swarming like bees. I could hear the sound of the bells again, and though the sound was unchanged, *I* was changed. For some reason, now it soothed me.

During this, I was aware that the paisley images I was experiencing were me, that somehow I had become them, or perhaps, that they had always been me, behind the *maya* of my own being. Since asparagus-ness was void of any self-awareness, this consciousness was very new. Permeating the Paisley was a sweet sensation of love, compassion, and joy. Half an hour passed easily in this state. The experience of the Paisley caressed me, assured me, calmed me. When the hammering of bells finally ceased, and the crush of people dispersed, I remained within the temple, and the Paisley continued. I was aware of the sights and sounds of the world, but in the foregound I saw this silent dance of formless paramecia swirling not before my eyes but in my brain. It was an orgasm that wouldn't stop.

Sometime later, I attempted movement, and observed myself walking gingerly across the temple yard. Outwardly, my appearance had not changed, but inwardly I no more resembled the Bruce Tolly Burkan of an hour before than a peacock resembles a wren. I would probably have been amazed at this metamorphosis, except that the state of consciousness I was enjoying precluded any such trivial reaction. New as it was, it was a familiar place, one that I recognized instantly. After all, it had been the singular object of my lifelong search. The form of my physical self was there, but inside was emptiness — emptiness, yes, but not a vacuum, because the Paisley was infinitely expansive. I walked, I spoke, I wandered outside of the temple grounds onto the streets of the village, but *I* was not the one doing these things. I was the watcher. The action came through me, not from me.

Eventually, I returned to my room, lay down and napped. When I woke before dinner, the Paisley was gone. Everything looked almost as mundane as it had before this extraordinary voyage into a new consciousness, but because *I* was changed, everything else was a little different, too. The sky was no longer flat blue, it was three-dimensional blue; leaves on trees were no longer just green, they were a thousand different shades of green. It was all quite subtle, but the profundity of this little difference hit me like a silent explosion. I did not speak for the rest of the day. I stayed alone, pondering what had taken place.

The next morning, our group prepared to leave for India. We were told that the trip to Sai Baba's *ashram* would take a few days. As we traveled, everything seemed dream-like to me. I felt as if I was in the activity of the group but not of it.

We arrived at the *ashram* on the Fourth of July. "Independence Day," I mused, "how wonderful!" Though this was the ultimate destination of our pilgrimage, everything that preceded our arrival at Sai Baba's had been so significant that even if the journey had not taken us there, I would have felt that I had benefited greatly. But, as Hilda had promised, the best was yet to come.

Unlike a temple, which houses only altars, an *ashram* provides living quarters for a Holy Man or Saint, also known in India as a "perfected Master." Although some *ashrams* have existed for centuries, Sai Baba's was erected in Putaparthi, where he was born in 1926, specifically to serve as his residence and as a center for his work. At the time Hilda brought us to see him, Sai Baba had already become the most renowned guru in India. His *ashram* was so large that it could accommodate thousands of people a day. Clusters of small cells with water spigots and toilets had been constructed to serve as housing, paid for by devotees who used them only at certain times of the year. In exchange for the use of a vacant cell, visitors were requested to donate fifteen cents a day. Meals were also provided for a nominal donation. These contributions helped not only with the maintenance of the *ashram*, they also helped to support its many community services, which included feeding the hordes of beggars outside its walls.

Indians consider it auspicious to be in the presence of a Holy Man. They call it receiving *darshan*. Sai Baba gave *darshan* twice a day by walking among the people assembled around the temple. The time was posted in advance. On each of the days we were there at least a thousand people gathered for the *darshan*, and often it was several times that number. People with deformities, illnesses, and disabilities begged for healings; curiosity seekers came with cameras; those who sought miracles waited and watched. I belonged to all three categories.

The first time I saw Sai Baba I was shocked. He was only about five feet tall. From pictures I'd seen, I'd imagined him to be far bigger. Nonetheless, since we all sat cross-legged on the ground while he walked among us, we were looking up at him. During the first *darshan* I attended, he paused above me and looked directly into my eyes. As I looked up at him, I was struck by the impression that his eyes were like cavernous holes — and *no one* seemed to be peering out. It was as if *nobody was in there;* he resembled an empty boat. A moment later, he moved on but even after he had passed, I felt a chill go up my spine. *Finally,* I saw a person without an ego, a human being residing in the state of *Constant Connectedness.*

"I was there," a voice screamed within me. "I recognize that place: Paisley!" In that instant I knew that Sai Baba wakes, walks, eats, speaks, and breathes while in this realm of consciousness. It's not something he chases after or experiences from time to time; it is his actual nature; he lives there. He shines like a beacon, reminding us of our potential, providing us with an example of something we need confirmed: that Divinity in human form is not a myth. It became easier for me to understand Divine humans like Jesus and Buddha because now I had encountered a human being who dwelled in that state of *Constant Connectedness* to the Universe.

SAI BABA

Since it was impossible for Sai Baba to give each person individual attention, it was suggested that people with specific requests hand the Master a letter as he passed through the crowd. Though he received countless envelopes twice daily, it was reported that he read every one. We were also told that Sai Baba remembered the face of each person who handed him an envelope, and that if he felt so inclined, he would talk to the writer of the letter the next time he gave *darshan*.

This was my chance. I wrote a letter describing the two things I wanted: freedom from pain, and to witness his magic! Hilda herself had been perpetually astonishing me since we had first begun the trip, and here was an opportunity to experience the Master with whom she had studied, the man she — as well as many doctors and research scientists — had called "a real magician."

Sai Baba accepted my letter on Monday evening. Tuesday morning he stopped in front of me as he wended his way among the people. He pushed the sleeve of his robe up past his elbow, and extended his open palm face down, about seven inches above my eyes. One moment, his hand was empty; the next, a small cloud puffed out of the skin of his palm, and from the cloud rained a sprinkle of grey powder, falling like a steady stream of salt. I caught the powder in my hands, my eyes transfixed on the skin of his open palm. When the materialization was complete, he motioned to the pile of powder in my hands, and commanded, "Eat it!" I shoved it into my mouth, and licked my hands clean. Sai Baba smiled and walked on. I was struck dumb!

Later, I speculated that the magic powder possessed curative properties, and anticipated a recovery from the nagging pain that tormented my body. But, to my chagrin, the pain immediately grew worse. Stabbing bolts of lightning began to lacerate my shoulders, neck, and arms. I bore them in silence. Weeks passed, and, though I went for *darshan* twice a day, the pain did not diminish one iota. I was stunned by the seemingly contradictory sequence of events. Eventually, the pain wore away my stamina, and I wound up spending most of my days in bed.

On one such morning, I awoke to find a huge spider spinning a web in the window of my cell. "So you live here too now," I thought. Watching the grace and the deft agility of the eight-legged creature mesmerized me, and I drew closer for a better look. The spider seemed to be aware of my nose almost touching its web. He paused before continuing. "So you're the creature I spent most of my life fearing," I remarked to myself with a smile. I realized how far I had come on the path of maturity. I wanted to reach out to pet the fragile being, but instead, chose to respect his delicacy and that of his silky web, and mentally caressed his belly with affection.

I lay in bed watching the spider, noticing how it seemed to entertain me and bring me joy. At that moment, my body was also in great pain, and I was struck by the ability of the brain to experience pain and serenity simultaneously. Furthermore, the serenity and joy were emerging from a situation that once would have created great fear in me. "The brain is such a mystery, such a marvelous wonder," I thought. "There is so much magic in the world, how often have I neglected to see it?"

Hilda had been working magic in my presence long before I met Sai Baba, yet often I had failed to perceive it for what it was. And Sai Baba's greatest magic was not his ability to conjure material objects from air, I realized, but his very nature itself. Despite the thousands of people constantly surrounding his house and pulling at him with demands, he remained sweet, loving, compassionate and patient. In the middle of chaos, I saw him standing composed and centered. He rose before the sun and retired after midnight. He consulted with government, doctors, clergy, giving selflessly to everyone, apparently indefatigable. Contrary to my former expectations, I could now see that the greatest magic, by far, was being able to witness a man who functioned continuously in the state of consciousness I had only tasted occasionally. Simply being near Sai Baba provided insights, understanding, and a healing of the mind.

As I lay there watching the spider, I felt acutely grateful. When

I considered how much pain the simple process of living had caused me for so many years, I could see that what I was now calling pain was really nothing by comparison. I found it ironic that I had traveled over ten thousand miles, hoping to receive a healing from pain that I had generally been able to live with, and now that I was in this distant place, I found myself writhing in an agony worse than any I had known since the accident. What a Cosmic joke! So often Sai Baba had been quoted as saying, "I don't always give you what you want, but I always give you what you need." Suddenly, life just seemed so absurd that I burst out laughing.

I decided to return to America the next day. The return flight took twenty-five hours, including numerous connections. As soon as I had started laughing in my cell at the *ashram*, the pain began to lessen; every day after that, more of it seemed to evaporate, until finally, after several months, it all but disappeared. Sai Baba had performed his magic on his terms, not mine, and in so doing, he taught me once again to "Let go and let God."

21

During the plane trip back from India, I experienced a renewed and empowered commitment to what I saw so clearly
as the purpose of my life: to contribute to the healing of the
planet in any way I could. Even though I perceived our planet
to be on a path toward destruction, and realized that our
cruelty to our fellow human beings was no less than it had been
two thousand years before, I still knew I could make a difference.

I saw that within my own country, large corporations were
jeopardizing the quality of people's lives in order to increase their
profits; pollution was virtually unchecked; resources were being
ravaged, and nuclear technology was producing lethal waste
in addition to unthinkably destructive weapons, and on a deep
level, I knew that if I wasn't going to be part of the solution,
then I *was* the problem.

Just as I could see that what I had done in my life up to that
point was the result of choices I had made either consciously
or unconsciously, I realized that my future was going to reflect
choices I would be making from that point on. Knowing that

everything I did would have an effect not only on myself, but on the world in which I live, I knew it was important to make choices from the highest level within myself.

Since war is just an outgrowth of fear and anger, if I acted and reacted from anger and fear, I would be contributing to the collective momentum that results in every war that's ever fought. If, instead, I acted with love and charity, I would be making a contribution toward solving the problem of war. I knew, of course, that simply saying this would not be enough; it would take commitment and work to follow through. But I also knew that once we decide to be the masters of our lives, and give Mastery our full commitment, we can write our parts any way we choose. In reaffirming the purpose of my life, I resolved both to live in accordance with the principles of harmony and charity and to make a determined effort to influence as many others as I could to do the same. After all, the survival of the planet is at stake.

Back in California once more, I felt excited, inspired — and happy. I didn't need any model for happiness; I had my own prior suffering to compare it to, and I was grateful for the enormous change. Instead of returning to Berkeley, I moved back to the marble quarry I loved so much, not into a trailer this time, but into a tipi. I didn't want to be a hermit again — in fact, quite the contrary: I felt that I could simplify my life in this setting, and at the same time, remain true to my commitment to serve others. I equipped the tipi with a battery-operated telephone answering machine, purchased several thousand feet of phone cord, and connected myself to the world via telephone. My heat source was a fire pit in the ground, and even though I spent the severest winter in 96 years within this canvas cone, I can't remember a more joyful, comfortable time in my entire life.

Voluntary simplicity nurtured me, and connected me to the root of my being. I was not accumulating too many of the things I knew couldn't fit into the narrow tunnel we all must eventually enter. It felt so refreshing not to be living a dozen service-levels away from natural resources. I gathered my own wood, and each time I needed to use a toilet, I went out and dug a hole. I kept trying to simplify my life: simplify, simplify, simplify. I could think of no better approach to living in these chaotic, changing times.

Personally experiencing the incredible benefits produced by simplification, I began to see what a remarkable course it would be for nations to pursue. The most reliable car is the one with the simplest technology. Once an automobile becomes burdened with countless gadgets and interdependent parts, there's that much more that can break down and confuse the mechanics. Our nation boasts of its complexity and high technology — yet we Americans suffer more heart attacks and cancer than any other nation on earth. Living in my tipi, and enjoying a greater sense of well-being and better health than I had ever known, I wondered if more people wouldn't choose to simplify their lives — though maybe not to the extent of living in a tipi — if they understood the price our society pays for its complexity in health problems, miserable relationships and spiritual starvation.

One evening, while the snow was thick on the tipi walls, smoke was curling up the open flap, and I was removing a bottle of Sake that had been warming in the fire, the telephone rang. Someone asked if I would do a workshop in Ukiah, California, a five-hour car drive away. Even as I was saying "Yes" into the telephone, something within me was beginning to feel unworthy.

After spending so much time with Hilda and Sai Baba in India, one of the things I knew about these Master Teachers is that they were completely free from fear. It was this freedom that gave them the power to create so much movement and healing. I also knew that for my whole life I had had an absolute terror that I had never discussed with anybody. Although I would teach and preach about the power of the mind to overcome anything, my secret fear had not yielded to therapy, hypnosis, meditation or affirmations.

This fear was a fear of heights. I couldn't climb trees, couldn't look out the window of tall buildings, couldn't even stand on a high ladder. As soon as I would look down, I would get dizzy, my knees would shake, then all my muscles would freeze, and I would feel paralyzed. Often I wouldn't be able to talk. The physical trauma resulting from this fear was every bit as intense as the worst pain I had ever experienced. While I was in India, it had never occurred to me to ask Sai Baba for a healing of this fear, and now I found myself back in America, about to teach the power of positive thinking, while living a lie. It simply would not do.

All at once I remembered the phrase: "Only those who risk going too far find out how far they can really go." The next thought in my brain was: "SKYDIVE!" The following morning I enrolled in a class to do just that.

The day of the course arrived, and I dressed without anxiety. I drove to the address I had been given and still felt calm. I was told that the format involved a two-hour instruction class, a one-hour practice session in jumping and falling, and, finally, the plunge. I looked around the classroom at the ten other students. Obviously, they all had their own reasons for being there, but it was my impression that I was the only one who was there specifically because of a fear of heights.

The classroom procedure was not intimidating. I simply paid attention to the information being presented. Our instructor ended the preparation by joking, "If the people look like ants — fine. If the ants are the size of people, your cord should have been pulled five minutes ago." Then we were taken outside to an area where we crouched on a platform, and practiced jumping into a sandbox. This is where the terror began to present itself.

Though the leap into the sandbox only involved a fall of three feet, my heart was pounding as I hunched my body on the wooden platform. I looked down at the sand three feet below, and suddenly realized what it represented: for all intents and purposes, it could very well have been 5,000 feet below me.

All the manifestations of my phobia blossomed. I began to sweat; my heart raced; my head throbbed. Dizzy, I clutched the railing with a ferocity that froze all the muscles in my hands.

Though a fragment of rationality reminded me that I was only three feet from the earth, my agony would not subside.

"Jump," came the instructor's command.

I was paralyzed.

"Jump," came the command again.

I felt weak.

"Jump," the voice called out a third time.

It is amazing how the human mind functions. There I was, only 36 inches away from the velvety sand, terrified. I jumped, outwardly silent, but releasing a blood-curdling scream inside.

"Again," came the voice.

The second time was easier.

Before I knew it, I was being harnessed into a parachute, and was boarding a plane. I was committed. Inside my head were a thousand voices: "What if the parachute doesn't open?" "What if my muscles freeze and I can't jump?" "What if I forget the proper way to land?" "What if. . .?" "What if. . .?" "What if. . .?"

Suddenly I became conscious of those two deadly words whipping me within: "WHAT IF?" There it was, the root cause of all my fears, the root cause of anyone's fears. . . two words! "WHAT IF?" An insightful flash come to my rescue, and I refused to allow the two words entry into my brain. Without them, I was safe; with them, I would be jelly.

Whether triggered by ancient memories of stories in books, dreams from long-forgotten nights, or just spawned by my imagination, the "what if" sequence of frightening images was the sole cause of all my terror. Seeing this, and handling it sucessfully as the plane ascended, were the breakthroughs that released the hormones I needed to soothe my knotted body. I was again able to think of God, perfection, and explicit trust in the unseen.

As I slid into the plane's open doorway and let my feet dangle in the whooshing air, I saw my fear again, this time poised on my shoulder like a pet monkey. I noticed that it had changed in nature. No longer was it piercing me with deadly talons; now it was merely cautioning me to use healthy respect for the precariousness of my position. It was counseling me to pay attention, remain alert, and be prepared for all eventualities. It demanded that I remember all I had been taught, and to appreciate the risks I was taking. I honored this new fear and noticed that it was simply the natural reflex of caution that every human needs to function at maximum capacity in life-threatening situations.

"Hi, old friend," I said to the considerate monkey.

"Jump," came the shout.

I visualized myself surrounded by a protective white light, and I jumped.

The moment my hands released from the doorway and I pushed my body into the open sky, Paisley enveloped me and I shot through space enjoying a sense of *Constant Connectedness.* No thoughts. No past. No future. I was NOW, and in the eternal "now" moment, nothing else existed.

The free fall whipped past outside of time. Within me, the Paisley danced, and Beethoven's Fifth Symphony pounded out the sound of Victory! As my mortal flesh plummeted downward, my spirit soared against gravity, and sailed for the stars. A tug at my armpits signaled the opening of the billowing canopy, and the approach to earth slowed to a comfortable pace. The silence was vast, the sensation unique. At an altitude of about two hundred feet, I readied myself for landing. Closer, closer, closer came the ground. A hundred feet, fifty, twenty, ten, contact. IT was over.

"Yeeee haaaa!" I bellowed, laughing uproariously. Free at last!

The next day I visited a skyscraper, and took the elevator to the roof. I had to test myself to see whether or not I was truly cured. I looked down. "My gosh," I thought, "I'm almost touching the ground." From where I had been the day before, no height seemed "high" by comparison. I breathed deeply, sensed once more my liberation, and realized there was absolutely nothing I couldn't do once I set my mind to it.

Liberated from the last of my haunting fears, I felt ready to tackle anything. The workshop in Ukiah turned out to be the best workshop I had ever given. Finally, I could use all my gifts 100 percent. God knew it, too, of course, and the next day I was presented with a new opportunity to serve: a phone call inviting me to be the master of ceremonies for a special show in New York to benefit the millions of people starving in Cambodia. I packed my red wig, my clown costume, my magic tricks, and left that night to join Leonard Bernstein, Bette Midler, Odetta, and the others who would be performing, grateful that my desire to be part of a network helping the world was manifesting into a reality.

As a result of the show, food and medical supplies were sent to Cambodia, and to refugee camps all along the Thailand border. Once more it was confirmed to me that we really can make a difference. I returned to California, feeling as if I had received a great deal more than I had given.

Since moving back to the marble quarry, I had begun performing the same services I had performed in Berkeley — visiting the hospitals, working with the Boy Scout troop, and assisting neighbors — only now in the nearby town of Sonora. After returning from New York, I began three new forms of service as well: working in a shelter for battered women and children; working with hospice patients, who were dying of terminal illnesses; and tithing ten percent of my income to charity. Because my schedule was in my own hands, and my workshops were on weekends, I was able to volunteer between twenty and twenty-five hours a week. I began to include in my seminars my belief that every able-bodied person can afford to tithe ten percent of his or her time to service. If forty hours a week are spent in earning a livelihood, most people can manage four hours of community service. These four hours of service are significant

The New York Times

THE NEW YORK TIMES, SATURDAY, MAY 31, 1980

The New York Times/Vic DeLucia

Children, including two young Cambodians, with Tolly the Clown, during the rehearsal for tomorrow's "Day of the Child" show. The proceeds from the events at the Beacon Theater will go to relief efforts for children in Cambodia.

'Day of Child' Benefit Is Set for Tomorrow

Ten-year-old Danielle Brisbois belted out the lyrics of "Tomorrow" before a rapt, young audience yesterday as she rehearsed for "The Day of the Child," a benefit scheduled at the Beacon Theater tomorrow for the children of Cambodia.

While Miss Brisbois, who appears on the "Archie's Place" television show, and others continue their rehearsals today, 50,000 free servings of ice cream will be distributed to children in front of the theater, which is at Broadway and 74th Street.

Produced by Kazuko Hillyer, head of the International Arts Center, which is serving as sponsor, the program will be a daylong triad of events.

A children's show, with clowns, mimes and the spotlight on young performers begins at 11 A.M. At 3 P.M., is "Interfaith Celebration of the Child," which will end with "Ode To Joy," the conclusion of Beethoven's Ninth Symphony. An 8 P.M. concert will include Bette Midler, Raul Julia, Walt Frazier and Odetta, among others.

Tickets for the children's show are $3 for children and $5 for adults. An "offering" will be made in the second show, and the suggested donation for the evening show is $10 to $50.

Yesterday, Mrs. Hillyer fended off countless requests for free tickets, saying all receipts would go to Cambodian relief agencies. "Even we're going to pay," she said.

to those who are served, and a rewarding experience for the server; they create friends, and improve the quality of life in the immediate neighborhood. As I learned for myself, we make a living by what we earn, but we really do make a *life* by what we give.

George Bernard Shaw remarked, "Some people see things as they are and ask, 'Why?' I dream things that never were and ask, 'Why not?' " I am now beginning to envision a perfectly harmonious world, free of hunger, prejudice, greed and war. Why not?

The third stage of growth, integration, requires that if we truly want peace in the world, we stop beating our own children. The "Do as I say, not as I do" approach is a losing mentality. We can all make a personal contribution to creating peace, love, joy, health, and prosperity on earth by living in accordance with these values — and sending positive thought forms into the Universe.

Most simply put, a "thought form" is a mental image. We don't usually admit to ourselves the enormous power of these mental images. But not admitting their power doesn't take any of their power away, it just prevents us from using the power productively. To think is to create; as thinkers we all live in a world of our own creation — and that is where "thought forms" get much of their power. I've learned that instead of thinking about the world as horrible, it's far more effective for me to think about the world as I'd like to live in it — and these thoughts automatically inspire me to actions that help to create that world.

By simplifying my life, by striving to live up to my commitments to give more than I take and to pursue *Attentive Awareness* in my everyday life, I am doing my best to contribute to this vision being realized. This means observing my own behavior, confronting barriers, working out my relationships with others, listening to their feedback to me and honestly making the effort to grow, even when it would be easier not to. It means being able to forgive others and to forgive myself. Healing the planet may be a long road, but a thousand-mile journey begins with one step. That one step is available to all of us.

The more activities I become involved in, the more organized I seem to become, and the greater the ease with which things move along. Even though I struggle at times, the more my ego lets go, the more my energy seems to flow. I often think of ego reduction as being synonymous with consciousness growth; if I want to see how conscious I am at any given moment, I can use *Attentive Awareness* to stand back and see how much ego is controlling me at that moment.

Once I became deeply involved in the process of integration, the fourth stage of growth, networking, followed automatically. It seems that our actions and dreams magnetize similar-minded people to work with us; like attracts like.

Of all the examples of this I've had in my life, one stands out as the most important. For years, people had asked me to sit down to write the story that you are now reading. So, in my tipi, between workshops and community service, I wrote the first draft. Not knowing what I had produced, I gave it to friends, hoping for some suggestions and feedback. One day my friend Shelley came up to the tipi to return the manuscript. She was radiant with excitement.

"You've got to show this to a woman I met in my mountain-climbing class!" she exclaimed. "When I asked her why she was taking the class," Shelley continued, "she said she was doing it to work on her discomfort about being in high places. I told her that I was reading your book, and I mentioned that you had gone skydiving to confront your fear of heights. Believe it or not, she also went skydiving to confront her fear of heights. Not only that, she just got back from India."

"India?" I interrupted.

"She was visiting Sai Baba!"

"Is she single?" I immediately asked.

"Yes. And guess what she does for a living? She teaches seminars in self-awareness!"

As soon as Shelley left, I reached for the phone and called her friend. As I dialed, I remembered the inner message I had been given — "Your mate is on her way" — and with the same sense of sureness and wonder with which I had received the message, I knew that the woman I was calling would be my wife.

22

Peggy had been teaching for years in Europe. She introduced consciousness work into the Scandinavian countries in the mid-seventies. Though American by birth, she was, in fact, of Nordic descent and has that type of look: tall and robust with broad shoulders, rosy cheeks and high cheekbones. Her most distinguishing feature is her unabashed, toothy grin. Her smile instantly inspired me to write a song about her.

We met in May and were married in October. My dream of having a family came true immediately since Peggy already had a son, Aaron, age eight, and a daughter, Taya, age eleven.

During Peggy's and my five-month courtship, I accompanied her to Europe where she was already scheduled to teach several seminars. I was astonished to find how akin her approach was to mine. Sometimes we taught together, sometimes separately. Both of us soon realized that we were much more effective as a team, that whatever power we possessed individually as teachers was amplified by our alliance.

When we returned from Europe in the fall, we noticed how

few husband and wife teaching teams there were. Soon we found out why.

Although our philosophies and teaching techniques were similar, there were times when we seemed chasms apart. When we had our first argument, it was in the middle of a seminar, and suddenly there was no way to separate Peggy and Tolly as teachers from Peggy and Tolly within our relationship.

Husbands and wives are often the best providers of sandpaper for each other's egos, because there are so many opportunities for their egos to rub against each other. Husbands and wives who teach together have the opportunity to experience this friction even more acutely, because they have to learn to share power and to be mutually supportive while they are in front of groups of people who are learning from them. If a husband and wife are teaching self-awareness, the experience becomes even more acute, because they are constantly forced to look at where their conflicts are stemming from, and where they are at odds with their own integrity. How can a husband and wife team of teachers be supportive of their students' growth if they compromise on the issue of their own growth?

After years of not having to share the platform with anyone, sometimes I found the pressure presented by this situation so uncomfortable — and the necessity of sharing power so difficult — that I wanted to run away. But when I realized that I was 100% committed to personal growth, I remembered that I had nowhere to run. If I was truly dedicated to eliminating my own ego games, and to coming from the highest possible consciousness in my life as well as in my teaching, how could I run away from the opportunity to see the games I was still playing, to observe the situations that still made me react?

Teachers often say that they learn at least as much as their students. I am particularly grateful for the lessons I've learned from teaching with Peggy, for the support we have both received from our students, and the even richer love that flows between

PEGGY DYLAN

us as a result of our working together and our commitment to working out whatever challenges that entails.

I am also grateful for the influence Peggy has had on the form our work has taken. Although her suggestions are often made in the most casual manner, they have resulted in changes that are profound and profoundly beneficial.

For example, one morning at breakfast, about a month after we were married, she turned to me and remarked: "Tolly, have you ever thought about teaching the firewalk as a seminar in itself?"

"Actually, no," I replied.

"It's such a powerful experience. It transforms people. I think it should be made available to as many people as possible. Think about it," she encouraged.

So in 1982, after teaching firewalking for years as part of other workshops, we created a four-hour firewalking workshop. The workshop was designed to assist people in overcoming fear and limiting beliefs, the two factors I observed to have been the most restrictive in my life and other people's lives. Our goal was that after having taken our four-hour course in firewalking, people might find themselves free, perhaps for the rest of their lives, of doubts and fears that up to that time they had allowed to hold them prisoner.

Recognizing the ambitiousness of this goal, we still felt assured of its possible attainment. The firewalk was the perfect metaphor to encompass all aspects of life, the full spectrum: from anguish to bliss. It was the perfect catalyst to raise fears and doubts as well as to challenge people's concepts about physical reality, what is possible and impossible.

The format we devised focused on the theme of "False Evidence Appearing Real" — F.E.A.R. We asked people first to describe the worst things they could imagine happening, and then to *expect the best.* Expecting the best, we explained, is more than just a good preparation for firewalking, it is a way of living our lives and performing at the level of our maximum potential.

The ability to walk on fire is a perfect example of mind over matter. There are two types of people, our firewalking students quickly find out, those who walk on fire, and those who don't. People have to decide for themselves which category they fit into. Everybody *can* firewalk; the question they have to ask themselves is, *"Do I think I can?"*

Before they come into our workshop, our students already know theoretically, at least, that walking over hot coals is possible. We're not there to convince them that it's impossible for them to get hurt. On the contrary, we tell them that according to Dr. Ron Sato, for example, faculty member of Stanford University Medical School and Director of a nearby burn Unit, human flesh momentarily exposed to 1200 degree heat would suffer third degree burns, charring the entire thickness of skin to a blackened carbon residue. Indeed, Dr. Sato himself has treated patients who *accidently* stepped on live coals and were so badly burned they required skin grafts. As for walking unharmed on hot coals, Sato said, "There's no logical explanation for it."

For those who want to busy their minds with a *possible* explanation, I offer the only information I've discovered that seems to have a bearing on how mind over matter may work in firewalking, and in other apects of life as well. For years, it was believed that there were only two glands in the brain: the pituitary gland and the pineal gland. Recently, however, researchers have discovered an entire network of glands that had previously been mistaken for lymph nodes. These glands respond to the thoughts in our minds and secrete substances called neuropeptides. Positive thoughts trigger the glands to alter the brain's chemistry one way, and negative thoughts stimulate a different chemical change.

When the brain's chemistry changes, it affects the chemistry of the entire body. Miraculous healings are more than likely the result of the mind influencing the chemistry of the body in a positive way. The simple act of stepping onto glowing coals demonstrates *the mind's knowledge that we will not be harmed,* and this positive thought alters the entire body chemistry in a way that permits the body to protect itself. Obviously, if people really think they will burn themselves to ash, they will not even take the first step.

Thus, neuropeptides may be part of *how* we literally do create our reality with our beliefs, how negative and positive thoughts actually translate into the physical world, starting with our own bodies. Firewalking begins with the first step; the first step begins with the thought. Whoever can't take the first step can't firewalk — and all it takes to firewalk is the first step!

At first people came to our firewalking workshops by word of mouth. Soon newspaper reporters began attending firewalks and writing about what we were doing. Magazine coverage followed. Before we knew it, thousands of people were signing up for our workshops wanting to walk on fire. In the midst of this, we started receiving invitations to appear as guests on television talk shows in both America and Europe. The inspiration that Peggy had shared with me over breakfast was fulfilling a need even greater than she had foreseen.

As we traveled across the country from one workshop to the next, we wrote our first book together, *Guiding Yourself Into A Spiritual Reality*. We got up every morning at 3 a.m. and meditated together for an hour. We then asked God to use us, and we put our pens to paper for another hour. The process continued for twenty days, at the end of which we had a book that contained the essence of everything we were teaching in our courses, including the firewalking workshop.

In the spring of 1984, we had to open an office to handle the huge public interest in our work. Again Peggy was the one with the clarity to see that in order to make firewalking available to the large number of people who wanted to have the experience, we would have to train others besides ourselves to teach it. So we began to gather people interested in teaching firewalking, inviting them to benefit from what we had learned, so that they, too, could pass on the incredible healing firewalking seemed to produce in people.

The prospect of overcoming fear has universal appeal, we've

observed. It magnetizes the curious, the spiritual, the conservative and the experimental, the healing professional and the professional in need of healing, the student and the teacher, people of every lifestyle, age, income level and educational background. Firewalking serves every person, and each is served in his or her own way.

I never really wanted to be known as father of a firewalking movement. However, dozens of people who studied with us now teach firewalking on their own and in their own style. Peggy's and my committment is really to teach people how to live and how to love. Our hope is that as people step through fear at firewalks, the planet itself is a step closer to peace. Like skydiving or head shaving, the firewalk pushes people beyond what they think are their limits. But unlike skydiving, firewalking has an aura of the miraculous about it. Whatever explanations are offered render the phenomenon no less of a miracle. Perhaps this is why so many people are drawn to it. Firewalking forces us to consider the miraculous nature of the universe of which we are all a part — and once we have firewalked ourselves, we can call to mind that sense of the miraculous as we go about our daily lives.

These past two years, the years I have been with Peggy, have been the most intense and growth-producing years of my life. I have been constantly walking on fire, and the rewards have been tremendous, both in the satisfaction I feel in having supported thousands of others in overcoming limitations, and in the joy I feel in my life. As I write this, Peggy and I are expecting our first child together. Every day we experience how our own thoughts are creating the lives we are living. Moment by moment, I get to see how *I* create my own reality — a reality for which I am very thankful.

23

Looking at who I am today and what I do as my work, I see that in some ways things haven't changed at all: I'm still traveling around the world performing magic — only now, the magic is personal transformation. Observing the similarities between my life today and my life years ago, when I began my search for happiness, I am reminded of the story of the stonecutter.

Long ago there was a man who had cut stone his entire life. His job was to chisel blocks from the side of a granite mountain, and send them to market for sale to masons and builders. One day, while the heat of the sun was pounding down on him, the king passed in a shaded coach, accompanied by his attendants and guards.

"Such a lucky man is the king," thought the old stonecutter. "In the heat of the day he rides about shaded and catered to by servants, comfortable and powerful. I wish I were the king," he said enviously.

Suddenly there was a crack of thunder, a flash of light, and the old man fainted. When he awoke, he found himself reclining on soft cushions, maidens were fanning him with palm fronds, and servants hurried before him pouring urns of hot water for his bath. He was the king!

Without questioning how this miraculous transformation had occurred, he took up his new role with pleasure and enthusiasm. One day, however, the stonecutter king ordered his coach to be readied and prepared for a journey into the forest. The sun was hot, and the king lamented that even the shade of the coach seemed to bring little relief from the oppressive heat.

As he rode, everywhere he was confronted by evidence of drought. "Here I am," he thought, "the powerful king of the land, and still I haven't the power to relieve the scorching effects of the sun. I always thought that no one possessed power greater than the king's, but I was wrong. The sun is the all-powerful one. I wish I were the sun."

Instantly, the king felt a whirling about his head, and when the dizziness subsided, he discovered that he was no longer a mortal man, but had actually become the sun.

"Ah ha," he beamed, "now I am the most powerful force there is!"

And so he spent his days radiating down on the earth, focusing his rays, burning the dry fields. As people fled his brilliance, protecting themselves by hiding in the shade, everywhere prayers were sent for rain.

Finally, after months of drought, the rains began. Try as he could, the sun could not penetrate the rain clouds, and water continued to fall to the ground, quenching the earth's thirst, and extinguishing the ravages of the sun's fiery scourge.

"Hmmmm," pondered the sun. "I thought nothing was more powerful than fire and heat, and yet now I see that next to water, I am helpless and impotent. It is far better to be a raging river than to be the sun."

Before another second lapsed, he was no longer aloft, but gurgling and rolling as he tumbled toward the sea, a rushing river. "Ah-h-h, now I am all powerful."

The ceaseless rain swelled his banks, and the river soon flooded the countryside. Homes were swept away in the water's fury, and countless people drowned in violent tidepools. The deluge dislodged huge boulders, sweeping them effortlessly along as it surged ever forward. "This is wonderful," thought the river, "nothing in my path can stand against me."

Suddenly, however, the river crashed against a granite mountain. Try as he could, the river could not budge nor erode the mighty monolith of granite.

"Oh no," the river said with chagrin, "the rock is more powerful than me. I should have chosen to be a mountain."

The wish, of course, was immediately fulfilled, and he became the mountain. "Now I am indestructible," he thought with satisfaction.

Several days later, however, to the mountain's surprise, a stonecutter appeared with hammer and chisel in hand. Whack. Whack. Whack. Slowly, but surely, huge chunks of stone were being carved from the mountain's side. Block by block, the stonecutter removed the granite and stacked it neatly for sale to the builders and masons.

"Indeed," observed the mountain, "this stonecutter has the power to take me apart in his own good time. I thought I was mighty, and yet this mere man is more powerful than me. I wish I was a stonecutter." And so he was.

In the past, like the stonecutter, I wondered why I wasn't lucky enough to have a better experience of life. Most of all, I wondered why I had to suffer so much. Now I see that the pain was all necessary; everything that happened to me was necessary to create everything that followed. I am thankful that the pain did not completely overwhelm me and that eventually I was able to move beyond it. One of the greatest inspirations in my life was my desire to change, and that desire was often prompted by pain. I finally realized that if I failed to learn from painful experiences, I was sure to repeat them. At that point I became conscious enough to ask, "*Why* am *I* creating my life this way?" And at that moment change became possible.

As people have served me by showing me a way out of pain, I hope that this book will serve others. As Hilda, Ram Dass, Ken, and Sai Baba have all been catalysts for me to learn from my pain, I hope that this book will be a catalyst for others to learn from their pain, too. We are all stonecutters, I believe, waiting for the illumination from inside that will let us know how much joy there really is in being ourselves.

"*After long searches here and there, in temples and in churches, in earths and in heavens, at last you come back. Completing the circle from where you started, to your own soul, you find that He, for whom you have been weeping and praying in churches and temples, on whom you were looking as the mystery of all mysteries, shrouded in the clouds, in nearest of the near, is your own self. The reality of your life, body and soul. That is your own nature.*"

—SATHYA SAI BABA

About the Authors

Tolly Burkan

Since the completion of this book, Tolly and Peggy have made a home for themselves in the Sierra Mountains of Northern California.

Mark Bruce Rosin

Mark Bruce Rosin graduated from the University of Chicago in English and received his M.A. from Yale University. He was Associate Literary Editor of *Harper's Bazaar,* Associate to the Vice President of Programming for CBS and Head of Motion Picture and TV Development at Talent Associates. He wrote the story for the movie "The Great Texas Dynamite Chase." After five years as Senior Editor of *Parents* magazine, he is now devoting full time to writing. His book *Step-fathering* is forthcoming from Simon and Schuster. He is currently co-authoring a book on real estate, *Zen to Zillions: The Consciousness Approach to Real Estate* and finishing a play. He lives in New York City with his wife and cat, and his two step-sons visit regularly.